TEACHING IN A
MULTICULTURAL SOCIETY

REXME CENTRE

JVg
LEM
(ra)

TEACHING IN A MULTICULTURAL SOCIETY

The Task for Teacher Education

Edited by
Maurice Craft

 **The Falmer Press**

A member of the Taylor & Francis Group

First published 1981

ISBN 0 905273 28 1

Jacket design by Leonard Williams

Printed and bound by Taylor and Francis (Printers) Ltd
Basingstone
for   .
The Falmer Press
(A member of the Taylor & Francis Group)
Falmer House
Barcombe, Lewes
Sussex BN8 5DL
England

CONTENTS

EDITOR'S PREFACE

This volume arises from the proceedings of an invited
seminar which took place at Nottingham University on
3-5 April 1981, under the auspices of the Advisory
Group on Teacher Education of the Commission for
Racial Equality. It was attended by some sixty
teachers from schools and further education, teacher
trainers, LEA advisers and teachers' centre wardens,
academic specialists and researchers, and members of
H.M. Inspectorate. Participants were drawn from all
parts of Britain, and were from both minority and
majority cultures.

The seminar, part of a wide-ranging development
programme being undertaken by the Advisory Group, set
out to explore the rationale and implementation of
multicultural perspectives in initial and in-service
teacher education, and to contribute to further
development. Papers were circulated in advance, and
each presentation was followed by a plenary discussion
session. The seminar sought a focussed and policy-
oriented style, although not to the exclusion of
important theoretical questions, and this
characterises the edited papers and discussion reports
which are presented here.

Warm thanks are due to all those who presented papers
and chaired the respective sessions, to Alma Craft who
recorded the various discussions, to Joyce Addington
for expertly producing the final typescript, and in
particular, to Frances Cooper who was responsible for
the administration of the seminar. May I also
acknowledge the support of the Commission for Racial
Equality which very kindly agreed to fund the seminar;
but responsibility for any views expressed lies with
the authors concerned.

Maurice Craft
Chairman
CRE Advisory Group on Teacher Ed.

August 1981

CONTRIBUTORS

IVOR AMBROSE joined HM Inspectorate in 1966, worked in the north-west and in E.London, and served on HMI national committees on multicultural education and educational disadvantage. Now has national responsibility in initial and in-service teacher education for the teaching of pupils with special needs.

DEREK CHERRINGTON is Reader in Educational Studies and Director of the Centre for Advanced Studies in Education, at City of Birmingham Polytechnic. In cooperation with the City University of New York, he is currently developing an International Centre for Multicultural Education based at the Polytechnic.

MAURICE CRAFT is Professor of Education, and Head of the Colleges Division, Nottingham University. In the early 1960s, he established ITT and INSET courses in multicultural education at Edge Hill College of Education, and has subsequently researched and established advanced courses in this field in Melbourne and in London.

JOHN EGGLESTON, Professor of Education and Head of Department, Keele University, is Chairman of the Editorial Board of the *European Journal of Education*, a consultant to OECD, and currently directs a Council of Europe project in multicultural education. Author of many publications in sociology of education.

JOHN GAFFIKIN studied at Manchester University, and subsequently took up employment in the milk industry before becoming a lecturer in further education. He was formerly Head of Business Studies at Brixton College of Further Education, and was appointed Vice-Principal of the College in 1975.

RAY GILES is a Professor of Education and former Chairman of the Department of Afro American Studies at Smith College in Northampton, Massachusetts. Currently on extended leave of absence, and working as Senior Research Fellow at the Centre for Advanced Studies in Education, Birmingham Polytechnic.

REG HARTLES is Chief Education Officer of the Outer London Borough of Ealing. He entered educational administration in 1965, having worked for some years in the field of teacher training, and prior to that he taught in schools and in further education.

ALAN JAMES, a Principal Lecturer in Education at Derby Lonsdale College of Higher Education, previously taught in multicultural schools in Huddersfield. He spent four months with Sikh families in the Punjab, and subsequently wrote *Sikh Children in Britain* (1974) Co-editor of *Multicultural Education* (Harper, forthcoming).

TUKU MUKHERJEE is Course Tutor to the advanced Diploma in Education for a Multicultural Society, at Southlands College, London. He was formerly a teacher of ESL and Head of Department in the Outer London Borough of Ealing, and a youth club and supplementary schools worker.

JOHN REX is Director of the SSRC Research Unit on Ethnic Relations, Aston University. Formerly Professor of Social Theory and Institutions at Durham, and Professor of Sociology at Warwick, his publications include *Race, Colonialism and the City* (1974) and *Race Relations in Sociological Theory* (1970).

HARRY TOMLINSON taught overseas, and in Billericay and Walsall, before his appointment to the headship of Birley High School, a multicultural inner city school in Hulme, Manchester. The school is featured in a BBC TV series about multicultural curriculum development, for use in in-service training.

SALLY TOMLINSON lectures in the Department of Educational Research, Lancaster University. Previously at Warwick University working on a major study of race relations in Birmingham with Professor Rex, she is currently researching into multi-ethnic secondary schools with David Smith of the Policy Studies Institute.

JEFF WHITE has been a Headmaster in Leicester inner city junior schools since 1974. A member of NAME, and a past member of Leicester's Community Relations Council, he lectures on the multi-ethnic primary school curriculum at the Leicester University and Polytechnic Schools of Education.

Chapter One

RECOGNITION OF NEED

Maurice Craft

This opening Chapter reviews the growing recognition of a need for the more informed preparation of teachers in a multicultural society, maps the response, and suggests some next steps.

The changing social composition of the nation's schools from the early 1960s has been reflected in a steady output of official reports, books and research papers which now comprise quite a substantial literature. It is a literature which reflects, on the one hand, a continuing confusion about overall aims in multiracial (or as it has since become known, multicultural) education, and on the other a continuing concern about the nature and extent of provision in schools and in teacher education. The two are naturally related.

To take the question of overall aims, put simply, are schools being asked to facilitate the speedy assimilation of culturally and linguistically distinctive pupils to the majority culture, or is there a more 'pluralistic' purpose? If it is the former, provision will be mainly concerned with the 'special needs' of immigrant or second generation children, with matters of language and literacy for example. If it is the latter, schools will be more concerned to acquaint all their pupils with the diverse origins of all members of our society, and to convey an appreciation of the intrinsic validity of different cultures. In this case, the curriculum for all pupils will be placed under review, not simply the curriculum for the newcomers. The emphasis in each case is clearly quite different.

This Chapter is based on written evidence submitted to the House of Commons Home Affairs Committee, in February 1981.

At the outset, with the arrival of the first wave of immigrant children from southern Asia and the Caribbean, the overall aim was strongly assimilationist. Immigrant children were deliberately spread throughout an Authority's schools. Some LEAs made efforts through withdrawal classes or special centres to cope with language and other basic skills, while others adopted a 'colour blind' policy and awaited full acculturation through the passing of time. The objectives for <u>teacher education</u> were therefore quite clear : those serving teachers working in schools with immigrant pupils should attend in-service courses on special needs, if available; but initial training need not do more than offer special options for students with a particular interest. However, pluralist views emerged quite early on. An increasing trickle of references to the need to prepare all children for life in a multicultural society began to appear, and with it the call for compulsory work in multicultural education in all initial training, in addition to specialist options and in-service training.

In this opening Chapter, the growing recognition of a need for the more informed preparation of teachers in a culturally plural society is examined through a review of the literature of the time. The confusion of overall aims and the consequent controversy in relation to policy and provision will appear and reappear. But perhaps the most insistent feature of the literature is the sheer repetition among the various commentaries. Whatever we have been trying to do, whether to assimilate our new citizens or to feel our way to a pluralist view, it is profoundly depressing to find the same kinds of recommendations for action appearing time and time again. The reasons for this would require a far more prolonged analysis than is possible here. But the failure to undertake even the beginnings of a rational clarification of aims, although understandable in such a politically volatile area, has given the impression of drift and may have contributed to the growing intractability of our problems in multicultural education. Undoubtedly, the slowness of education (and particularly of teacher education) to respond to the changing social composition of the schools, has been related to the uncertainty about aims referred to above. But the preoccupation of teacher educators with the revolution in the structure and content of teacher training since

1960 has possibly also been a factor. A third element must relate to the attitudes of teachers, and the wide variation in the degree to which they have perceived multicultural education as either a clear or a desirable aim for schooling.

This chapter therefore begins with a brief review of early expressions of need in initial and in-service teacher training, and an appraisal of more recent reports. This is followed by a detailed examination of such evidence as exists regarding provision in initial and in-service training, from the 1960s to the present; and then by a brief discussion, first, of comments which have been made about teacher attitudes and the take-up of in-service courses, and second, of the initial *vs* in-service debate. Finally, I have included a number of suggestions for future policy.

Early Expressions of Need

Patterson's (1963) study of W.Indians in Britain was one of the earliest reports to call attention to the key role of education in preparing children for membership of a multicultural society, and to urge the full participation of teachers in reviewing a largely ethnocentric curriculum. "Somehow it should be possible to find space in the training college syllabus for a course in race and human relations", she wrote. But in fact it took us a little time to find space, and to begin to think beyond a more limited, 'special needs of immigrants' perspective. Bowker (1968), writing of the "obvious need for teachers to be as fully equipped as possible to understand the problems faced by members of immigrant minority groups", commented on "the sad fact ... that many students pass through our colleges of education unaware that such problems exist". In 1969, E.J.B. Rose's landmark study of British race relations confirmed this gloomy picture. "Institutes of education", he reported, "were slow to respond to the need for teachers prepared to work with immigrant children, including E_2L work", and an Authority like Birmingham built up its own team of peripatetic specialists. Elsewhere, groups of teachers came together voluntarily in workshops and conferences to exchange practical ideas and 'emergency do-it-yourself' techniques.

In 1970, Bhatnagar's research in a multi-ethnic school called attention to the fact that many immigrant

children arrive in Britain with very different
educational and social backgrounds.

>"Some of them come from rural, pre-industrial
>cultures and move straight into the classroom in
>the middle of the industrial Midlands. The point
>that they may need different teaching methods,
>educational aids, and classroom organisation
>seems to have been completely lost on their
>teachers. Few teachers have been trained to cope
>with immigrant children /̲ and ̲/ ... special
>courses ... will have to be provided on a far
>more extensive scale than they are now".

The Schools Council reported in 1970 on immigrant
children in infant schools (a study of 11 LEAs), and
observed that little short-course provision for infant
teachers had so far been made, although things were
rather better in areas of high concentration where a
specialist adviser had been appointed. This enquiry
also reported that "many colleges do not yet do enough
to prepare their students for this work", despite the
strategic importance of tackling special needs at this
early age, and the likelihood that many young teachers
would take up first posts in these areas (Schools
Council 1970a). (Virtually the same comments were
offered five years later by the Bullock Report in
respect of the training of nursery and infant teachers
(DES 1975, para. 20.15)).

All these observations are typical of the
'compensatory' view of the earlier days, when many of
the ethnic minority children in our schools were born
overseas. But they have been echoed down the years
both by those concerned about the special needs of
minority group children, and by those advocating
change in the curriculum for all children in a
multicultural society. The Select Committee on Race
Relations and Immigration (1969), for example, took in
both objectives:

>"We would like to see every college of education
>in the country teaching its students something
>about race relations, and the problems of
>immigrants. To say that there is no need to
>educate all students about such matters because,
>as one college has said, 'very few of our
>students go into schools where they are likely to
>meet mixed classes', is to miss the point.

Teachers should be equipped to prepare all their children for life in a multicultural society". (Op.cit., para 214).

Townsend's (1971) landmark study, a national survey of the LEA response to the changing situation in the schools reported that, "repeatedly on visiting schools with immigrant pupils, research officers heard comments from LEA officers and head teachers about the lack of preparation of many teachers for a new and difficult task," even staff in special language centres and classes. In their second major survey, this time of the internal organisation of 230 primary and secondary schools with varying proportions of ethnic minority pupils, Townsend and Brittan (1972) again concluded that an outstanding feature of the staffing of these schools was their lack of adequate preparation for teaching in multiracial schools. "Neither initial nor in-service training is meeting the urgent needs of teachers for greater knowledge of immigrant backgrounds and of suitable techniques for use in the classroom", they said. And going on to a broader and less problem-oriented view:

" ... there is a valid argument that not all students will become teachers in multiracial schools. There is an equally valid argument that all students in colleges of education are expected to become teachers in a multiracial Britain, but this did not seem to have been reflected in the courses of the probationer teachers in the sample". (Op.cit., pp. 138-139).

And so it goes on. The HMI Survey of the educational progress of immigrant pupils in 54 secondary schools in 16 LEAs, published in 1972, expressed disappointment at the schools' response, and expressed the hope that an increasing number of LEA in-service courses would offer teachers the guidance required; and that young graduates, in particular, would be offered the appropriate training in their PGCE courses (DES 1972a). The 1973 Report of the Select Committee on Race Relations and Immigration, recommended that "students at colleges of education should be made aware that, wherever they teach, they will be doing so in a multicultural society", and that "this should be reflected not so much in special courses, but throughout the training, more particularly in such aspects of it as the sociology of education" (op.cit., para. 114); they also recommended an expansion of in-service provision to meet the special needs of minority group children. In 1974 came the CRC/ATCDE Report, a significant policy statement signalling the end of the 'education of immigrants' approach, as such a large proportion of minority children were now indigenous Britons, arguing for a more pluralistic view and outlining detailed programmes of work at initial and in-service levels (op.cit., 1974).

More Recent Reports

The Bullock Report, on language teaching appeared in 1975, and devoted a long chapter to ethnic minority children, making numerous observations on relevant needs in initial and in-service training with particular reference to language teaching, ethnocentric school books, and attitudes to dialect variations (DES 1975). In 1977 the 'Green Paper' which followed the former Prime Minister's call for a public debate on education in his Ruskin College speech, re-iterated the concerns which had already been expressed a decade earlier. "The Secretary of State", it reads, "shares the misgivings of those who believe that too many entrants to the teaching profession have inadequate experience and understanding of the world outside education, including its multicultural and multiracial aspects ...", and it recommended a high priority for in-service work "in relation to the special problems of multiracial schools, immigrant communities and schools in deprived inner urban areas" (DES 1977). Another 1977 reminder of what still remained to be done was produced by the Community Relations Commission in its Report to the Home Secretary on urban deprivation and racial inequality. This report cited the views of a sample of teachers who "felt inadequately trained for their work in multiracial schools, and many felt they received insufficient support or guidance from the local authority". There was also "a high degree of demand for an increased level of initial and in-service training of teachers to give them the skills needed to teach in multiracial schools" (CRC 1977).

In 1979 came the publication of an HMI enquiry into developments in the B.Ed. degree course, a study of 3 polytechnics and 12 colleges. This reported that the treatment of education in a multicultural society was 'superficial or non-existent'; and "the compulsory elements of most courses did not ... bring students towards much awareness of the special needs of certain categories of children, in particular those with a cultural background different from that of the majority or those whose learning was otherwise handicapped". Expertise it seems was usually present in most colleges, but it was made available chiefly in optional courses. "Yet such needs as these," the report observes, "are likely to be encountered by any teacher in his first post" (DES 1979b). In the following year the Inspectorate undertook a further sample survey into initial teacher education, this time focussed quite specifically on multicultural aspects. Although not yet published, the findings (reported in Chapter Nine below) are hardly encouraging, almost half the institutions perceiving little relevance in multicultural issues, and PGCE courses having barely responded at all. This survey was complemented in 1980 by that of Professor Eggleston and his colleagues at Keele University into in-service teacher education in a multiracial society, and this is reported in Chapter Five below. At the end of their detailed enquiry the researchers concluded that, "Our investigators have left us in no doubt about the fragmentary and incomplete provision of in-service teacher education for a multicultural society. Indeed, it is non-existent in many areas and in none is it wholly adequate" (op.cit., 1981).

In 1981 came the first report of the important Schools Council enquiry into multicultural education, a large-scale survey which has reviewed the work of all LEAs in England and Wales, and has also examined a sample of secondary schools and raised syllabus issues with Examining Boards. The Survey reported data from 94 LEAs, and some 525 schools in areas of varying concentration. In its recommendations, the report places heavy emphasis on the need for in-service courses for LEA officers and teachers in areas of varying concentration of minority ethnic groups, including the "consideration within other in-service courses of the implications of a multi-ethnic society", and it advocates appropriate action by the DES, schools and by the Schools Council and professional associations. Training institutions are urged to consider the implications of a multi-ethnic society for the preparation of all students; to provide specialist options; to offer a range of in-service courses; to develop 'as a priority' appropriate award bearing courses; and to give positive consideration to ways of recruiting staff and students from ethnic minority groups (Schools Council 1981).

The major HMI surveys of primary and secondary education also appeared in 1978 and 1979, and neither paid a great deal of attention to multicultural aspects. But the primary survey indicated that "more might be done to make all children aware of other beliefs and to extend their understanding of the multicultural nature of contemporary society" (DES 1978, para. 8.55); and the secondary survey similarly noted that "reading specifically selected for ethnic minorities, or more generally to reflect the fact that ours is a multicultural society, was seen in only a small proportion of the schools" (DES 1979 a, para. 6.2.19). The much-heralded DES paper, *The School Curriculum* (1981a), however, went considerably further in its recognition of changing school needs. School curricula, it stated, "must appropriately reflect fundamental values in our society", noting, "First, our society has become multicultural; and there is now among pupils and parents a greater diversity of general values" (op.cit., para 2c); and going on to comment on the implications for religious education, and for modern language/mother tongue teaching. Understandably, perhaps, (as these three reports are all concerned primarily with school curricula and organisation), the implications for teacher education are not drawn out, and they are left to the teacher educators themselves to appraise.

For a more direct up to the minute comment on teacher training we must turn to the 'Rampton Report' on the education of W. Indian children, which was published this summer (DES 1981b). This declared quite bluntly,

> "The evidence we have received from all sources, including schools and teachers, LEAs, students and parents presents an overwhelming picture of the failure of teacher training institutions to prepare teachers for their role in a multiracial society. In very few institutions is a grounding given to all students in how to appreciate and understand the experiences and cultures of ethnic minority pupils, or of how to help ethnic minority parents who may not have much personal experience of this education system" (op.cit., p.60).

The situation with regard to the in-service training of experienced teachers presented 'a more positive picture', the Committee felt; but even so, few LEAs were reported to have an Adviser with special responsibility for multicultural education, and provision seemed extremely variable across the country. The Report recommended a 'fundamental reappraisal' by teacher training institutions of their policy towards multicultural education, and appropriate action by HM Inspectorate and by LEAs in respect of in-service work and the recruitment of more W. Indian staff.

The same critical stance was taken by the even more recent Report on racial disadvantage, published by the House of Commons Home Affairs Committee in August 1981. On reviewing the evidence, the Committee felt that progress in teacher education had been slow, and that "it is no longer acceptable to wait for the complex administrative structure of teacher training to come to terms in its own good time with the challenge presented by the multiracial classroom" (op.cit., para. 138). Permeation of initial training courses by the recognition that Britain is a multiracial society is what is required, the Committee urged, not the provision of an 'optional extra', and particularly so in PGCE courses which now provide half the output of new teachers. But at the same time, initial training 'should not skimp' on specialised language skills, or provide them only in urban institutions, for young teachers are obviously being trained for a national market and are likely to meet ethnic minority pupils at the outset of their careers. The Committee's recommendations (- "and we declare our intention to monitor implementation of these recommendations in particular" -) included a training-the-trainers programme, and action by validating bodies.

So much for a brief review of what has been said about the preparation of our teachers for work in a multicultural society, over the past twenty years. Sometimes the special needs of minority group children have been stressed, at others there is a broader concern for the education of all children in all areas. Mostly the comments have been directed at Colleges of Education, but more recently provision in the PGCE, which includes Universities, has been noticed. At first, an assimilationist view was generally adopted, but latterly a more pluralistic concern has appeared. Throughout it all, however, emerges the depressing repetition of inadequacies in initial and in-service teacher education; it is an indictment not simply of central and local government for failing to give a lead or to make resources available, but also of teacher educators, course validators, and schools, for failing to respond more imaginatively and with a greater sense of urgency. None of us can escape responsibility for our collective shortcomings. Certainly, it may be argued that the system is huge; that it operates on a decentralised principle with responsibility delegated down to the individual class teacher on most professional issues; and that change for these and many other reasons is therefore bound to be slow. Nonetheless, the return on a substantial investment of time, expertise and money expended in large-scale surveys, the compiling of reports, the sitting of major committees, and the like, has so far been pathetically small.

Provision in Initial Teacher Training: early surveys

The reports summarised above have sought to outline the extent of initial and in-service provision and to give some indication of its effectiveness. But only a few of these studies offer more than generalisations, and for a more detailed picture of the measures which have actually been taken we need to consult other material. The following sections will seek to fill out the picture somewhat, but the available data is scanty.

Possibly the earliest relevant material is provided by the 1966 surveys carried out by the former National Committee for Commonwealth Immigrants and H M Inspectorate. Both surveys indicated that "relatively few colleges were yet running or intending to introduce optional courses of a substantial nature in the field of immigrant education" (DES 1971b). The NCCI estimate was 15%, and information from both surveys suggested that "perhaps 3 out of every 10 colleges included in its curriculum some discussion of immigrant education or of life in a multiracial society", usually by means of a very brief course and often of a single day's duration. Most of these colleges were in areas of high concentration. These early surveys were followed by several national conferences which reflected the NCCI's concern that initial training institutions had a responsibility to offer some provision for all students, and preparation in greater depth through special options for some (op.cit).

A second NCCI survey, paralleled by a further HMI enquiry, followed in early 1969, and these both suggested that 30% of the colleges - most in areas of high concentration - were then 'deeply involved' in this work, compared with the 15% in 1966. In addition, a further 60% (compared with 30% in 1966) were offering a certain amount of more general work. But University departments of education appeared to be doing little. The situation thus seems to have improved markedly by 1969. In 1972, Townsend offered a little data in respect of the 596 primary and secondary probationer teachers in the sample of 230 schools in which be was investigating provision for immigrant pupils. Of these, only 11% reported having received any specific preparation for teaching in multiracial schools (Townsend & Brittan 1972, Table A.33), a less encouraging picture than that reported for 1969.

Present Provision in Initial Teacher Training

Between the late 1960s and the present time there was a revolution in initial teacher education in the public sector. Closures, mergers and diversification (i.e. the development of non-vocational degree and diploma courses alongside the teacher training courses) have radically altered the map, and to attempt any comparison of then and now is probably risky. However, what can be said of the present situation? We can gain a crude idea of the current provision in initial teacher education by an analysis of courses listed in the authoritative handbook (NATFHE 1980). This indicates that only some 4 institutions (out of more than 80) in England and Wales specifically mention course offerings in this field, in programmes leading to the (initial) B.Ed., B.A., B.Sc., B.H., B.Th. or Dip.H.E.; and only one out of 92 institutions offering the P.G.C.E. On the other hand, it is probable that multicultural aspects arise in the many courses in sociology, social studies, social administration, community studies, urban studies and so on, which are currently offered. Indeed, many lecturers might claim that they offer a pluralistic presentation in core studies in education. Again, it is possible that students in many courses in initial training may opt to undertake practical work, essays or major studies in the multicultural field. Nonetheless, this is a curiously small proportion in view of the reported findings for 1966, 1969 and 1972. Three recent and as yet unpublished studies go beyond the crude statistical data of the NATFHE Handbook, but although helpful, none can be said to offer anything approaching a comprehensive analysis. The first enquiry is a national survey conducted in 1979 at Birmingham Polytechnic for the Commission for Racial Equality, and reported in Chapter Four of this volume (Giles & Cherrington 1981). This reviewed all courses concerned with multicultural education in Colleges and Institutes of Higher Education, Polytechnics and Universities, whether as discrete units or as elements of other courses. It therefore included all initial training courses (B.Ed., P.G.C.E.), in-service named awards (Dip.Ed., M.A., M.Ed.), and diversified degrees (B.A., B.Sc., B.H.).

Giles and Cherrington's data offers a slightly more encouraging picture, and suggests that getting on for half the 64 Colleges, two-thirds of the 31 Polytechnics and one-third of the 52 Universities approached, offer something in the multicultural field. Furthermore, a number of institutions indicated that further courses are in preparation or in the course of validation, and the authors feel that the total number of offerings may be expected to grow. The offerings included discrete courses and elements of courses, but they were found to be by no means always compulsory. Some were about Britain as a multicultural society, others aimed at developing specific competencies for teaching in multi-ethnic schools. The report notes that we still need to know much more about the policy of individual institutions with regard to multicultural education, to staffing, resources and course evaluation, but it presents no data on these several aspects. Nor do we know how many institutions offer a pluralistic perspective in all they teach. Overall, the findings are difficult to compare with those of earlier studies as, clearly, categories have changed substantially in the meantime. But although, on this data, it seems possible that provision in PGCE courses for graduates has improved, we still have nothing like the 90% coverage of college courses which was claimed in 1969.

A second, as yet unpublished, study which was completed in 1980 and which also offers a little relevant data is that of Jones and Street-Porter who undertook a pilot enquiry into the implications for initial and in-service education of educational disadvantage. This was one of the last endeavours of the Centre for Advice and Information on Educational Disadvantage, and was carried out under the guidance of a steering committee which I was invited to chair. The task was a sizeable one, and with the (part-time) authors working to complete a report before the closure of the Centre, the outcome is claimed to be no more than indicative. Some 1300 courses or parts of courses leading to initial and advanced awards in teacher education were scanned, 180 of which were relevant to educational disadvantage were selected and of these, 21 were subjected to close examination. The authors found many of these offerings to be optional; and their overall assessment is that work concerned with educational disadvantage appears in about one-third of all initial training courses, (and in about 10% of all in-service long courses). They also briefly examined LEA short-course provision, and were involved in discussions with LEA advisers, H.M.I., lecturers, educational researchers and social workers, so their assessment of both initial and in-service work is discussed together here.

Jones and Street-Porter found that the greatest number of courses, or elements of courses, devoted to educational disadvantage in fact addressed themselves in some way to the issue of education and race, and the tutors they consulted were of the opinion that 'multicultural', 'multiracial' or 'multi-ethnic' courses have increased in recent years. Such courses are generally found in or near major urban areas, and like Giles and Cherrington's Report for the C.R.E., the authors report that it is in these areas that expansion is taking place. They also corroborate Giles and Cherrington's finding that a number of relevant proposals are in preparation or in course of validation. But they note that their discussions indicate a certain amount of local variation. A number of longer in-service courses in multicultural education have failed to recruit or have been discontinued, for example, - because of "poor quality of teaching, outdated source materials and information, a changed general outlook on the issue and consequently changed needs as perceived by the classroom teacher", (a point taken up later). Reasons for an increase in interest were equally diverse. Staff changes have also affected the starting/closing down of courses, as have the loss of L.E.A. secondments.

As noted by Giles and Cherrington, the C.E.D. Report found that most courses concerned with ethnicity appear to be optional, and that they tend to fall into two categories: those aimed at the development of special skills for working in multi-ethnic classrooms, and those which emphasise a broader preparation for teaching in a multicultural society - the two elements already noted in many other reports. The authors comment on the rather vague aims of these courses, and on the absence of any coherent body of theory underpinning their construction; and they note the importance of specialist teachers' centres both in providing short courses and in servicing initial training courses in multicultural education. In their recommendations, Jones and Street-Porter note the need for theoretical clarification on matters of education and race in teacher education, for an updating of bibliographies, and for more discussion of issues relating to dialect and to bilingualism. So the C.E.D. report appears to corroborate some of the findings of Giles and Cherrington, and adds a little more detail. But it must be noted that this enquiry took account of multicultural education in the context of a broader study of teacher education provision in respect of educational disadvantage. This is obviously only one aspect of the question, and on the broader issue of how far all teacher trainees are currently being prepared for work in a culturally plural society, the report says little.

The third very recent report on multicultural provision in initial teacher training is that considered in Chapter Nine of this volume. This was an HMI survey in two-thirds of all public sector initial training institutions, carried out during 1979-80, and in the words of HMI Ivor Ambrose, "The overall picture ... is not a particularly bright one". Perceived improvement in some institutions is off-set by deterioration or limited provision in others, the whole suggesting a "somewhat dormant state". Nonetheless, 30 out of the 46 B.Ed. courses considered had included some reference to education in a multicultural society at some point in the compulsory elements of the degree, (although the PGCE situation was far worse). Again, most institutions offered a relevant B.Ed. option, and a few offered a relevant main subject such as urban studies.

It will be very clear that the data arising from these various surveys hardly amounts to more than the crudest indication of what is actually happening in initial teacher training in the area of multicultural education. We know little of the methodology employed by the various researchers, and of the extent to which their categories and classifications are comparable one with another. As for comparisons with the earlier surveys, as already suggested, this is extremely risky for institutions, awards and staffing have all altered since the 1960s. What then can we conclude? If we take only the Giles and Cherrington report, and if it is regarded as no more than indicative and in no way definitive, the situation can hardly be regarded as completely satisfactory. Perhaps one-half of all initial teacher training institutions have made some provision (this was also the DES estimate in their evidence to the House of Commons Home Affairs Committee in June 1980)[1], but some of it is optional. And then again, is the real figure more or less than one-half? The CED Report suggests that it may be as low as one-third, while HMI Ivor Ambrose's figures indicated that something is being done in perhaps two-thirds of the institutions in his sample.[2] The Rampton Report was derisive:

"No teacher training institution appears to have succeeded in providing a satisfactory grounding in multicultural education for all of its students. Many offer optional courses in such subjects as English as a Second Language, and Education for a Multicultural Society, but these often take place too late in the course and are over-theoretical, and, in some cases, are little more than token gestures. The great majority of students are thus entering teaching having

---

1   House of Commons (1980), para.30.

2   In their evidence to the House of Commons Home Affairs Committee, the NUT reported a January 1981 survey of all teacher training institutions, which revealed that of the 67 responses so far received, only 15 reported that all students would encounter some work on education in a multicultural society, 'and even fewer replies mentioned a compulsory element'. Most of this work occurs in multi-ethnic areas. (House of Commons 1981b, page 141).

received little or no guidance on how to adopt a broadly-based approach to education which takes full account of the presence of ethnic minorities in our society". (Op.cit., p.61)

This seems a harsh judgement. Maybe there has been some progress since 1966, and it is possible that a number of new proposals are currently in process of validation. Nonetheless, the 'optional' aspect is an imponderable; and with an increasing proportion of initial teacher education now taking place in PGCE courses where multicultural elements seem likely to be fewer, the situation may not have improved very much during the 1970s. 'Can do better' might be an appropriate end-of-term report.

Provision in In-Service Training

What about in-service training? According to E.J.B. Rose (1969), there were in 1963 no in-service courses in English as a Second Language for teachers of immigrant children, and no relevant books or materials. By 1967, according to the Schools' Council's 1970 report on the education of socially disadvantaged children in secondary schools, there was still no University diploma or short course "relevant to compensatory education and the problems of schools in priority areas" currently running, although courses in remedial education, counselling and curriculum development were seen as being directly relevant. As to DES, LEA and other courses, the picture was "hardly more encouraging": 0.09% of the total were devoted to "teaching socially handicapped pupils", and 9% of the 7,700 teachers responding to an ongoing enquiry stated that they were involved in this work. The report concluded that in-service provision was far from adequate, and as in several such enquiries it also noted that it seemed "doubtful whether the recognition of need for such provision among teachers was as widespread as it ought to be in view of the seriousness of the problem" (Schools Council 1970b). Of course, this report was concerned with the overall question of educational disadvantage. The DES report on *The Education of Immigrants* in 1971 was more specifically relevant. This stated that between 1964-67, only 1% of teachers in English County Boroughs had attended courses in the teaching of immigrants; and that a mid-1968 survey by HMIs working in the 40-45 areas of high concentration indicated that about half

of the LEAs concerned had organised relevant courses.
One-term courses on the teaching of English as a
second language had been under-subscribed, and several
had therefore been discontinued. Three one-year
advanced diplomas in linguistics were also then in
existence, but as with the one-term courses, demand
had "not been overwhelming". This 1971 report
discussed these matters in detail, devoting its
longest chapter in fact to teacher education, and
offering many practical comments on the considerable
scope for further development (DES 1971b).

Townsend's survey of LEA provision for immigrant
pupils at the beginning of the 1970s brought the HMI
figures up to date and presented the national picture.
He reported that 41 out of 146 LEAs were offering
courses in this field (i.e. 28%, and 58% of those LEAs
which were making special arrangements for immigrant
pupils). The great majority of these courses were
part-time, short courses. But even in those LEAs
offering in-service courses, respondents pointed out
"the considerable difficulty of interesting secondary
school teachers in courses on the education of
immigrant pupils, other than teachers from English or
remedial departments" (Townsend 1971). In the second
major N.F.E.R. survey, on the internal organisation of
schools with immigrant pupils, published in 1972,
Townsend and Brittan reported that of the 4,853 staff
in all 230 schools in their sample, only 7% had
attended any relevant in-service courses (i.e. 15% of
primary teachers, and 3% of secondary), during the
three years prior to the survey. And again there is a
comment on teachers' attitudes: "... There does appear
to be a failure on the part of teachers either to
recognise their needs or to make them known. And even
when courses such as the DES courses on immigrant
education are made available they are frequently
under-subscribed" (op.cit., 1972).

As to in-service provision at the present time, the
current DES handbook of long courses indicates that
only 4 out of some 80 institutions in England and
Wales specifically mention a multicultural element in
their programmes for the in-service B.Ed. degree. But
many institutions offer courses in the sociology of
education, language, urban and community studies,
ethical, philosophical and political issues, and
curriculum studies in this award, and multicultural
perspectives might occur here or elsewhere. As regards

advanced Diplomas, only 10 out of 320 currently listed
are specifically related to multicultural education.
But there are also others concerned with urban
education, educational disadvantage, community
education, counselling, and bilingual education; and
Diplomas concerned with language, R.E., sociology,
curriculum and other specialisms - as well as more
general Diploma courses - which might also include
relevant matter or special options, or be presented
from a pluralist standpoint. As to higher degrees, no
single M.A./M.Ed. taught course anywhere in England
and Wales appears to be devoted to multicultural
education according to the D.E.S. list, but one is
known to be about to start at St Mary's College,
London, and a second is in course of planning at
Nottingham University. Here again, taught higher
degrees in urban education (only two, in London), in
E.F.L., language, community education, sociology of
education etc., as suggested above, may be relevant;
and of course, many M.A./M.Ed. courses may offer
special options. So clearly, the overall situation is
difficult to quantify.

The current provision of _short_ courses for experienced
teachers by LEAs, tertiary institutions, the Schools
Council, subject associations and other bodies is very
extensive, even at a time of economic stringency, and
here again, there is no easy way of assessing the
multicultural input. A little evidence is offered by
the annual review of short courses put on by H.M.
Inspectorate (DES 1980b), and it appears that of 91
courses to be mounted in England between April 1981
and March 1982, only five are to be devoted to topics
such as 'teaching and learning in multicultural
primary schools'. Of the 10 courses in Wales, two are
concerned with Welsh language issues. But again, there
is no way of assessing the extent to which
multicultural aspects might be included in the short
courses which are to be offered on assessment, social
studies, religious education or elsewhere. The HMI
sample survey in two-thirds of the public sector
teacher education institutions in 1979-80 (reported by
Ivor Ambrose in Chapter Nine) found that in-service
courses, mostly of an award-bearing kind, appeared in
'fewer than half' of the sample institutions, and in
some regions nothing was offered even where a
contribution was being made at the initial level. As
HMI Ambrose writes, "... the best examples of good
practice were to be found in cases where an

institution had developed a balanced programme of long and short in-service course provision in close cooperation with its Local Authority's advisory service in multicultural education".

But it is to the Schools Council and Keele surveys which both appeared this year that we must turn for an overall view of the current INSET situation. The Schools Council enquiry reviewed present in-service provision in all LEAs in England and Wales. Less than one-third of the 94 LEAs responding to the survey reported that they provide courses on multicultural aspects of education, and half of these LEAs were in areas of high concentration, (on the face of it, a similar proportion to that reported a decade earlier by Townsend). It appears that almost all these courses were for experienced (and not specifically for newly appointed) teachers, almost all were short part-time courses, and less than 10% were school-based. On the other hand, 42 LEAs reported that a multicultural dimension was included in other in-service courses. As to problems encountered in developing INSET courses in multicultural education, the difficulty mentioned most often was that of attracting teachers who were thought to need them most; several said that in practice their courses involved "preaching to the converted", or that it was difficult to recruit teachers from schools with few ethnic minority pupils. A number of LEAs also referred to lack of available expertise, including specialist advisers, specialist members of ethnic minority communities, or additional funding to develop appropriate INSET programmes (Schools Council 1981). Professor Eggleston has more to say on all these points in Chapter Five of this volume, where he reports on the latest large-scale survey of in-service teacher training in multicultural education. The 'fragmentary and incomplete' provision he refers to, not wholly adequate in any area and non-existent in many, leads his team to make a wide-ranging series of recommendations: the DES should facilitate an enhanced spread of provision and of take-up, so that coverage depends less than at present upon 'predominantly independent institutional initiatives'; LEAs should give clearer recognition to in-service work in this field, and to teachers who have completed such courses; schools also need to make better use of expertise gained through in-service courses; and

course providers need to consider the development of a
national information network, and a reappraisal of the
content and staffing of their offerings (op.cit.,
1981).

Finally, the Rampton Report, which, perhaps rather
surprisingly, made little comment on in-service
provision other than to say that it presents 'a much
more positive picture' than that in initial training,
and indicating that progress had been made in a number
of LEAs and in school-based work. Some Authorities
were reported to have appointed an Adviser with
special responsibility for multicultural education,
but the Committee felt that the wide variation in
relevant advisory provision was inadequate; and the
Committee also recommended that LEAs review the
effectiveness of their induction programmes for
probationary teachers. The appointment of specialist
Advisers is, in fact, a rather crucial matter and was
a particular point of comment in the very recent
Report by the House of Commons Home Affairs Committee.
As the Report put it:

> "The practice, in Avon and Leicestershire, of
> having no Adviser exclusively concerned with
> multicultural education, and indeed in Avon of
> linking the function of advising on multicultural
> education to that of advising on English and
> Drama, underestimates the significance of
> multicultural education in these areas".
> (Op.cit. (1981), para. 146).

It will thus be clear from this brief review of in-
service opportunities for practising teachers that, as
with initial training, there is a dearth of hard data.
The available information is fragmentary, there are
serious problems of definition, and one study is not
fully comparable with another. Nevertheless, when
exercising all due caution and regarding the data as
merely indicative, there does seem to be a degree of
consistency in the low level of provision - even given
the narrow, 'problem-oriented' nature of the
perspective adopted. The 28% of all LEAs offering
courses reported by Townsend in 1971 becomes less than
one-third of the 94 LEAs who responded to the 1981
Schools Council survey, for example; it is indeed far
from certain that there has been any substantial
improvement in coverage over the past decade. There
is also evidently much variation of course provision
from region to region. Nor do we know anything very

much about the actual effect on teachers' attitudes
and professional expertise of such provision as has
been made; or whether, with the changing social
composition of ethnic minority children (there are now
few _immigrant_ children in our schools) the content of
'special needs' courses has kept pace. A further
question is whether the next steps should be less in
terms of 'courses' than of school-based curriculum
development, involving a whole school staff in each
case. This would require a quite different pattern of
resourcing and evaluation, and is touched on again
below. All in all, the Rampton Report's final refrain
seems to be fair comment: "... in-service provision,
whilst rather more encouraging $\angle$ than ITT $\angle$ could
still do far more ..." (op.cit., p.72).

The Attitudes of Teachers

There is also a degree of consistency in the various
studies reported here in what has been said about
teacher attitudes. In 1970, the Schools Council's
report on _Immigrant Children in Infant Schools_ had
noted the paucity of relevant in-service provision;
but it had also observed that teachers seemed to be
largely unaware of such support and resources as then
existed (op.cit.). In 1972, the HMI survey of the
educational progress of immigrant children in 54
secondary schools in 16 LEAs commented:

> "The findings of the survey indicate clearly that
> the majority of schools in the areas concerned
> could undertake much more positive thinking and
> constructive action in matters relating to the
> linguistic, intellectual and social needs of
> second-phase immigrant pupils."

While much had been achieved in the area of language,
the report felt that a greater awareness by teachers
of the all-round, continuing needs of immigrant pupils
was required, and that "this pre-supposes willingness
on their part to learn more about the difficulties
experienced by such pupils, to make themselves more
knowledgeable about their backgrounds and to seek
advice from and cooperate with their specialist
colleagues in the field of ESL and with their head of
English department". (DES 1972a).

This last comment is firmly in the 'compensatory'
tradition that we have noted. In 1973, Townsend and
Brittan produced a Schools Council report exploring a

broader theme - the extent to which <u>all</u> children were being prepared for life in a multicultural society - as well as seeking information on more specific provision. Their findings, in a sample of 435 primary and secondary schools in areas of varying concentration were encouraging:

> "There appears to be a considerable majority of headteachers in all types of school, whether multiracial or not, and whether in immigrant areas or not, and of heads of departments in multiracial secondary schools, who consider that one of their aims should be to prepare pupils for life in a multiracial society".

But as the report also pointed out, (a) this degree of support for multiracial aims was not so fully reflected in the actual syllabuses, nor (b) could it be ignored that very few teachers had at that time attended relevant courses, ("and some national courses have been cancelled for lack of applicants"). (Op.cit.).

In 1974, the Community Relations Commission's report on in-service education, based on a survey of 100 teachers in London, the Midlands and the North, found that teachers are "becoming more aware of the need for support and information to help them with their own particular situation in urban areas". But they felt that <u>school-based</u> work would be the most effective, and there seemed little evidence in current provision "that this concept of in-service training for multiracial schools had been understood or accepted by the majority of course providers. Examples of the involvement of the entire school staff in discussion of principles and policies of multicultural education were rare", (CRC 1974). With this report we have a first clear indication that the attractiveness (and effectiveness) of in-service provision in multicultural education may depend not only on teacher motivation but also on the techniques used. In 1976, Brittan reported on yet more of the NFER multicultural research programme, this time an in-depth enquiry in 25 schools and involving 510 teachers. Her conclusions were that "one is led to suspect ... that the needs of multiracial schools were not being fully understood and recognised by the teachers involved, nor therefore the need for teacher education"; and she, too, noted that in recent years a number of courses on multicultural education organised by the DES, University Institutes and LEAs have been cancelled for lack of support, "... thus calling into question the nature and effectiveness of such courses" (op.cit.).

More recently, Professor John Eggleston's Keele enquiry (reported in Chapter Five) has called attention to the question of teacher response. As he writes, "course providers regularly advised us of 'sluggish' demand, unfilled or even cancelled courses; some LEA advisers justify low provision on the grounds of low demand", and he goes on to consider problems relating, for example, to communication, finance, professional support, and professional recognition. More recently still, the January 1981 survey of multicultural provision in all teacher training institutions carried out by the NUT, reported that 'a very disturbing feature' was the number of institutions which reported a drop in the take-up of in-service courses for serving teachers; but this was blamed by institutions on the 'lack of possibilities for secondment by LEAs' (House of Commons 1981b, p.143)

On the basis of such evidence as is reviewed here, it would be facile to offer definitive comments on the attitudes of teachers towards participation in multicultural in-service work. Nor should this be attempted in isolation from an examination of teacher participation in other forms of in-service training in education. There is in any case a huge teaching force distributed throughout many regions and a wide array of teaching institutions, so easy generalisations should be resisted. But the repetition of the theme of teacher awareness and involvement in courses must be noted nonetheless. Indeed, my own experience in providing advanced in-service courses in urban and ethnic studies since the mid-1960s would support these general findings. If we are also to take note of other recent comments on teacher attitudes in this context, there would seem to be a dimension of INSET here which merits fuller attention from researchers and in-service providers. The Rampton Report, for example, speaks of the 'unintentional racism' of teachers, "... stereotyped or patronising attitudes towards W. Indian children, which when combined with negative views of their academic ability and potential, may prove a self-fulfilling prophecy" (op.cit., page 70). In a different vein, Stone (1981) has criticised the 'self-esteem' school of research which leads "teachers /to/

act more and more like social workers and consequently neglect their primary role of 'instruction'," to the particular disadvantage of W. Indian children (op.cit.). Attracting teachers into in-service discussion of such issues is clearly of some importance.

But the few comments on the form of in-service work in this field which have appeared in this section are also important. As suggested earlier, perhaps school-based approaches should now be given fuller consideration.

Initial or In-Service Training?

Finally, the question of whether appropriate provision should be made at the initial or in-service levels. There is perhaps more than an element of futility in this debate, for it is difficult to see how either can be dispensed with. But it has been another recurring theme during the past decade. The 1969 Select Committee report drew a distinction between preparing all students for teaching in a multiracial society, and teaching them how to teach immigrant children. Where the latter involves the teaching of English as a second language, the Committee felt, "This kind of training is proabably best given to already experienced teachers by means of various types of in-service training courses", (op.cit.). As a member of the ATCDE National Executive and of a UCET Standing Committee at that time, I can personally recall this being the view of both bodies. The James Report on teacher education appeared in 1972 and while recommending that "an understanding of the multicultural nature of society should feature in any general education", it tended to give greater emphasis to in-service training. Firstly, not all colleges could offer appropriate practical experience in multiracial schools, and secondly, not all young teachers would encounter these special needs in their first appoinments (DES 1972b).

These kinds of views were strongly represented by the ATCDE to the 1973 Select Committee which agreed that "the right time for more specialised training is when it is needed, in areas where problems arise", namely via in-service training (op.cit.). The Select Committee's report was followed in 1974 by a Government White Paper which endorsed the emphasis on in-service training, but allowing also for relevant basic courses for all students and special options for some (DES 1974). The 1977 'Green Paper' suggested that a number of localised 'centres of scholarship and professional expertise' in multicultural education should be fostered, but this document also tended to emphasise the priority of in-service training (DES 1977), as did the Government White Paper on *The W. Indian Community* in the following year (Home Office 1978). In 1979 the prevailing ideology was still in evidence, and the HMI survey of developments in the B.Ed. degree course reported that "in more than one college, it was stressed to the visiting panel that the B.Ed. course had been envisaged in the expectation that a period of planned induction would make good the acknowledged deficiencies of the initial training course." No amount of re-timetabling could produce more hours in the day (DES 1979b).

To the cynic all this has been an elaborate exercise in buck passing, but this would perhaps be too harsh a judgement. That relatively so few initial training institutions have incorporated basic material on Britain as a multicultural society for all students (by re-designing existing courses, not adding new ones) is certainly remarkable. That so few have developed specialist options in depth, utilising local schools, is less surprising, given the location of many colleges at that time. That the in-service challenge was, it seems, taken up by neither short-course providers nor teachers in great numbers is also rather puzzling, given the needs at that time. As Jones (1977) has observed, the colleges have always fed a national labour market, and until the spread of ethnic minority communities had begun to grow, there was a case for arguing that only a small proportion of young teachers would have need of special skills in their first appointments; and as teachers are professional workers, they could hardly be directed into in-service courses where they seemed to be in need of them (op.cit.). Even so, the profession has until recently been very mobile, and the special needs of immigrant children could perhaps have been expected to be encountered within five years of first appointment, if not before. As regards compulsory INSET, it has since become increasingly common for 'whole-school' in-service work to take place during term-time.

Policies

This paper has sought to review some of the main themes in the development of appropriate teacher education strategies in respect of multicultural education, over the past decade or so. At the outset, it was suggested that a confusion of aims and objectives has bedevilled constructive development. If the education of ethnic minority children is perceived as a 'problem' requiring special skills, then preparation in some depth is needed, either through special options in initial training (in institutions in areas of high concentration) or through in-service training. If, on the other hand, the education of such children is perceived in a pluralist perspective, this would be relevant to the entire curriculum of initial teacher education; students would have considered bicultural and bidialectal strategies, would have discussed ethnocentric curricula, and however unpracticed in terms of specialised classroom techniques, would have been unsurprised by the range of cultural backgrounds encountered on first appointment. As we have seen, the predominant educational perspective in the early years was assimilationist, and the emphasis was accordingly on INSET. The perspective is changing, partly because of pressure from ethnic minority communities who wish to retain a distinctive cultural identity as black Britons, partly because minority group children can now be found in very many parts of the country, and partly because a very large proportion were born here anyway and the initial problems of adjustment no longer exist.

However, as suggested earlier, despite this fundamental ambiguity of aims and objectives, it is difficult to explain, fully, the incomplete success of the 'compensatory' approach. Why has INSET coverage been so variable, and why has teacher take-up sometimes fallen short? It is easy to forget that most educational innovations are slow to take root, and multicultural education is probably no slower than the development of coordinated pastoral care and counselling systems or the establishment of closer home-school links. Each of these has taken a comparable period to gain acceptability amongst teachers and trainers. But neither has the political urgency of multicultural education, and if the depressing repetition of recommendations brought out in this paper may be said to reflect a lack of creative leadership in central and local government, in teacher education and in the schools, it ought also to be interpreted as a spur to more expeditious development in the next five years. What form ought such development to take?

We have first to recognise a number of <u>structural features</u> in contemporary teacher education which offer both limitations and opportunities. These are sketched below, beginning with the B.Ed. and PGCE awards, and going on to consider long and short in-service courses, school factors, regional organisation, and lastly the question of national leadership. First, then, initial training in colleges and polytechnics (i.e. the B.Ed. degree):

- despite its slowness to adapt to multicultural needs, initial teacher education has been substantially expanded and then very rapidly contracted over a fifteen-year period, with very remarkable resilience. The level of courses offered has risen from the two-year Certificate of Education to four-year B.Ed. (hons.) and other first degrees, PGCE, advanced diploma and in some places, taught masters degrees. During expansion, new departments and forms of college government developed, but this was followed by diversification, mergers and closures, and redundancies. Thus, <u>low morale</u> will, understandably, be a factor in any proposal for change

- on the other hand <u>the standard and range of staff, library and other resources</u> now available is far higher than was the case in the late 1960s, and there is no reason to suppose that institutions will fail to respond given the opportunity to clarify aims and objectives, in a more pluralistic climate of opinion, and with a school population including a substantial proportion of black Britons

- it is true that falling enrolments have greatly reduced the appointment of new lecturers with recent school experience, and in any new development available expertise <u>may need to be supplemented</u> by close liaison with LEAs, schools, and ethnic minority communities

- closures may also have affected the number of urban colleges available for relevant practical work. But <u>attachments to urban colleges</u> is already practised in several regions

- the B.Ed. degree with its modular structure lends a new flexibility to the <u>development of specialist options</u>

- the ending of college validation by many Universities places a <u>greater responsibility upon the CNAA</u> in any programme for enhancing multicultural education in many initial training institutions.

Secondly, initial training for graduates (i.e. the Postgraduate Certificate in Education):

- there has been a radical change in the national balance of 'concurrent' and 'consecutive' initial teacher education, with a much greater proportion of young teachers now coming through the PGCE route. This lends even <u>greater urgency to a review of PGCE provision</u> for multicultural education

- the same development suggests that a <u>review of multicultural elements in first degrees,</u> which feed PGCE courses, be undertaken, through normal academic interchange.

Thirdly, in-service trining for practising teachers (long and short courses):

- current economies have substantially reduced one-year secondments and even day-release for school teachers, giving <u>greater importance to school-based work during term time</u>

- the radical decline in new appointments in schools <u>gives greater importance to in-service education</u> compared with initial training.

Fourth, school factors:

- the loss of one-year secondments will <u>reduce</u> <u>the number of teachers available as change</u> <u>agents</u> in schools, those who have studied relevant issues in depth at in-service B.Ed., diploma or M.Ed. level

- the reduction in promotion opportunities <u>may</u> <u>encourage young teachers to choose</u> <u>multicultural development</u> as a career avenue, if LEAs offer appropriate encouragement.

Fifth, required organisation:

- Since the demise of Area Training Organisations and the absence of any subsequent Government initiative, the coherence of regional planning has suffered considerably. But <u>intelligent regional</u> <u>coordination</u> in course planning and resourcing is clearly essential in any new development in multicultural education in both initial and in-service training, for individual institutions and LEAs will vary in their capacity to mount courses or school-based initiatives. This situation will be sharpened by current economies in INSET and similar constraints in initial training.

Sixth, national leadership:

- the closing of the Centre for Advice & Information on Educational Disadvantage has removed a potential source of national leadership in the field of multicultural education, and perhaps <u>places a greater</u> <u>responsibility</u> upon the <u>Department of</u> <u>Education and Science</u>.

Bearing in mind the limitations and also the opportunities presented by the structural features outlined above, it seems to me that the following elements would need to be considered in any programme of development for teacher education. They comprise three groupings - those concerned with initial training, in-service training, and regional/national coordination.

(a) <u>initial training</u>

- despite the greater importance of in-service education which follows from several of the structural changes indicated above, it seems essential (i) to continue with development at the initial level, both in terms of <u>core courses</u> and of <u>specialist options</u>; and (ii) to take account both of the continuing <u>special needs</u> of ethnic minority children, and also of the need to educate <u>all children</u> for life in a culturally plural society

- but there is also a need for institutions to consider a systematic <u>review of all they teach</u>, for a more pluralistic awareness could render any additional core courses unnecessary.

Both these proposals would be aided by the exploration of aims and objectives, and the new knowledge input suggested in para.(c) (last two sections) below.

- <u>attachments</u> to other institutions for students' practical work should be utilised by those in areas of low concentration; and limited <u>staff/library resources should be supplemented</u> through liaison with other tertiary institutions/LEAs/schools, utilising such regional machinery as exists

- representatives of <u>UCET, PCET, CNAA and all Universities validating</u> initial and in-service named awards should be called together at an early date to consider multicultural education in the training of teachers

- the special problems of the <u>PGCE and its feeder courses</u> should be the subject of an early national conference

- further <u>research into ways of increasing ethnic minority participation</u> in initial training should be undertaken at an early date.

(b) <u>in-service training</u>

- such regional mechanisms as exist should

review the field, and call together a
<u>representative working party in each region</u>
to stimulate the development of relevant
short and long courses

- modes of <u>school-based development during
  term-time</u> should be explored, as a first step
  in generating more participative modes of in-
  service training in this field

- further <u>research into teacher attitudes</u>
  towards multicultural work should be
  undertaken at an early date

- tertiary institutions should ensure that
  <u>multicultural options are available</u> in in-
  service B.Ed., diploma or taught masters
  degree courses, and that part-time study is
  possible.

(c) <u>regional and national co-ordination</u>

- H M Government is urged to <u>publish early
  proposals for regional planning in teacher
  education</u>, to facilitate these and other
  developments

- such regional machinery as exists <u>should
  offer all possible support</u> to initiatives in
  multicultural education in each region

- the <u>DES should initiate</u> as many of the
  proposals in paras (a) and (b) above as
  require a national lead, working through such
  other agencies as seem appropriate in each
  case. The DES should also take steps to
  <u>facilitate the dissemination</u> of relevant
  current developments by The Schools Council,
  the Commission for Racial Equality and other
  bodies, if only by means of a national
  newsletter

- the DES (through such other agency as is felt
  appropriate) should set on foot <u>an evaluation
  of progress</u> in teacher education, in two
  years' time

- the DES should initiate an <u>exploration of
  aims and objectives in multicultural
  education</u>, to be published either as an HMI

working paper, or as the outcome of a commissioned seminar or special consultancy*

- the DES (through such other agency as seems appropriate) should set on foot the establishment of a series of 4-6 week courses for lecturers and advisers in initial and in-service training, as <u>a training-the-trainers exercise</u>, to be based for a limited period in several regional centres. These courses would seek to clarify aims and objectives, introduce members to relevant areas of knowledge and professional skill, bibliographies and other resource materials.

These proposals represent a personal view, and were submitted in evidence to the House of Commons Home Affairs Committee in February 1981. All assume that there would be appropriate consultation with representatives of ethnic minority communities.

Of the sixteen suggestions put forward, the last - training the trainers - seems to me to be the single most important step which might now be taken in stimulating development in initial and in-service teacher education; for unless there is to be a more systematic and purposive approach to increasing multicultural expertise in the training system at large, change will continue to be slow, patchy and superficial. Some twenty years have passed since the first recognition of need, the beginnings of a realisation that a multicultural society requires a more sophisticated professional competence of its teachers, and all the evidence suggests that we have so far made only limited progress. The task for teacher education is only too clear.

---

* A paper now seems likely to be published by the Schools Council towards the end of 1981. An exploration of multicultural aims and objectives in <u>teacher education</u> is expected to be undertaken by the CRE Advisory Group on Teacher Education.

REFERENCES

Bhatnagar, J. (1970), Immigrants at School, Cornmarket Press

Bowker, G. (1968), Education of Coloured Immigrants, Longman

Brittan, E.M. (1976), "Multiracial education: teacher opinion on aspects of school life", in Educational Research, 18, 3.

Community Relations Commission (1974), In-Service Education of Teachers in Multiracial Areas, CRC

CRC/ATCDE (1974), Teacher Education for a Multicultural Society, CRE

Community Relations Commission (1977), Urban Deprivation, Racial Inequality & Social Policy, HMSO

DES (1971a), Potential & Progress in a Second Culture, HMSO

DES (1971b), The Education of Immigrants, HMSO

DES (1972a), The Continuing Needs of Immigrants, HMSO

DES (1972b), Teacher Education & Training ('James Report'), HMSO

DES (1974), Educational Disadvantage & the Educational Needs of Immigrants, (Cmnd. 5720), HMSO

DES (1975), A Language for Life ('Bullock Report'), HMSO

DES (1977), Education in Schools: a Consultative Document (Cmnd.6869), HMSO

DES (1978), Primary Education in England HMSO

DES (1979a), Aspects of Secondary Education in England, HMSO

DES (1979b), Developments in the B.Ed. Degree Course HMSO

DES (1980a), Long Courses for Teachers 1981/82, DES

DES (1980b), HMI Short Courses for Teachers, April 1981 - March 1982, DES

Eggleston, S.J. et al (1981), In-Service Teacher Education in a Multicultural Society, mimeo., University of Keele

DES (1981a), The School Curriculum, HMSO

DES (1981b), West Indian Children in our Schools ('Rampton Report'), HMSO

Giles, R. & Cherrington, D. (1981), Multicultural Education in the U.K.: a Survey of Courses and Other Provision in British Institutions of Higher Education, CRE, (unpublished)

Home Office (1978), The West Indian Community, HMSO

House of Commons (1980), Racial Disadvantage, Minutes of Evidence, 26 June 1980 (DES), HMSO

House of Commons (1981a), Racial Disadvantage, 5th Report from the Home Affairs Committee, Vol.1, HMSO

House of Commons (1981b), Racial Disadvantage, Appendices, Vol.4, HMSO

Jones, C. (1977), Immigration & Social Policy in Britain, Tavistock

Jones, C. & Street-Porter, R. (1980), Educational Disadvantage: Implications for the Initial & In-Service Education of Teachers, Centre for Educational Disadvantage, (unpublished)

NATFHE (1980), The Handbook of Degree and Advanced Courses in Institutes/Colleges of Higher Education, Colleges of Education, Polytechnics, University Department of Education, Lund Humphreys

Rose, E.J.B. et al (1969), Colour and Citizenship, Oxford University Press

Select Committee on Race Relations and Immigration, (1969), The Problems of Coloured School Leavers, HMSO

Select Committee on Race Relations (1973), Education, Vol.1, HMSO

Schools Council, (1970a), <u>Immigrant Children in Infant Schools</u>, Evans

Schools Council (1970b), <u>Cross'd With Adversity</u>, Evans

Schools Council, (1973), <u>Multiracial Education: need and innovation</u>, Evans

Schools Council, (1981), <u>Multi-ethnic Education: The Way Forward</u>, Schools Council

Townsend, H.E.R. (1971) <u>Immigrant Pupils in England</u>, NFER

Townsend, H.E.R. & Brittan, E.M. (1972) <u>Organisation in Multiracial Schools</u> NFER

Townsend, H.E.R. & Brittan, E.M, (1973), <u>Multiracial Education: Need & Innovation</u>, (Schools Council Working Paper 50), Evans

Chapter Two

AIMS AND OBJECTIVES

John Rex

In this paper, Professor Rex considers some of the overall aims and the more specific objectives of multicultural education, in the context of a fundamental concern for equality of opportunity.

For someone who is engaged in sociological research in the field of race relations, the sort of debate around which this kind of symposium is apt to centre has a distinct sense of unreality about it. On the one hand, we may hear from those who share certain basic liberal democratic assumptions about aims in relation to the education of ethnic minorities, and who imagine that these aims can be realised within the existing system without difficulty, if only we can clarify the means to be used. On the other hand, there are those, who, starting from a position of political radicalism or sociological determinism, may suggest that the system is totally recalcitrant, has malign purposes, and could only be used to realise the aims of multicultural education if it was wholly transformed as a part of a more radical social revolution. Such a debate gets diverted into rhetoric in which the policy-oriented moderates discuss their ideal aims in what is in a strict sense an ideological way, while the radicals posit even more remote and unreal aims, which in their political utopia are thought of as realisable without limit.

I have some sympathy with the radicals in this kind of debate, because, as a sociologist of race relations, I am well aware both of the depth of racist commitment in our culture and of institutionalised racialist discrimination in our social and political practice. I do, however, have a minimal commitment to reformism in that I believe that the debate about ends in this sphere is not solely and simply ideological; and that within the rhetoric of the policy makers, there are matters on which they can be pinned down, and I see my role as a sociologist as one of spelling out the institutional consequences of their professed commitments. I would argue that it is possible to be a radical without falling into the trap of what

amounts to political quietism, or of believing that
the only possible terrain for change is to be found in
social change in wider political contexts than that
represented by the school.

In seeking to make a realistic contribution to this
symposium, therefore, I would lay emphasis on three
areas of discussion: firstly, a consideration of
whether there is within the debate about aims,
rhetorical though it is, a more limited set of
objectives which can be fought for within the existing
system, even though the precise spelling out of these
objectives might excite opposition which would remain
quiescent so long as the debate remains on the level
of rhetoric; secondly, a look at the actual
transactions, of a social as well as a purely
educational kind, which go on in the schools; and,
thirdly, the development of a critique of what now
passes as multicultural education.

The Debate About Aims

The starting point of the official debate lies, of
course, in the tension between the first statement by
the Commonwealth Immigrants Advisory Council in 1964,
and the statement by Roy Jenkins in the run up to the
passing of the 1968 Race Relations Act. The
Commonwealth Immigrants Advisory Council stated that,

> "... a national system of education must aim
> at producing citizens who can take their place
> in society properly equipped to exercise
> rights and perform duties which are the same
> as other citizens. If the parents were
> brought up in another culture or another
> tradition, children should be encouraged to
> respect it, but a national system cannot be
> expected to perpetuate the different values of
> immigrant groups" (op.cit.1964)

Roy Jenkins, on the other hand, is quoted as saying
that the overall process of immigrant absorption
should be seen "not (as) a flattening process of
uniformity, but an equal opportunity accompanied by
cultural diversity in an atmosphere of mutual
tolerance" (Patterson 1969).

Many critics have pointed out that although these
statements indicate a move from crude assimilationism

to a more sophisticated notion of integration and
cultural pluralism, the Jenkins approach was
vague, impossible to operationalise, and still aimed at
maintaining the majority culture intact. For my own
part, my reaction to the Jenkins statement was that
while it described the relatively genteel processes of
adjustment amongst the middle classes of Golders Green,
it had little relevance to the situations of class
conflict and oppression in which most immigrants found
themselves.

The critics of the Jenkins statement, however, have
often implicitly or explicitly posited an alternative
to his general goal that I think to be highly
unrealistic. This is that it is possible to fight in
Britain for a completely multicultural society in
which the various immigrant cultures and languages
come to have equal status with traditional English
culture, and, indeed, that that culture itself should
change and adapt so as to include foreign elements. I
would by no means argue that this aim is not a worthy
one and I would find it rewarding and enriching to
live in a society with a complex culture of this kind.
But, if it is seriously suggested that cultures should
enjoy equality in Britain in the same way as say,
Flemish and Walloon culture coexist equally in
Brussels, or French and English culture in Quebec, I
can only say that such situations rest upon a
political balance underlying them which could never
conceivably be brought about in Britain, where what we
are discussing are essentially minority cultures.

To say this, however, is by no means to say that
multiculturalism has no place in Britain or in its
educational system, or that what has already been
achieved is satisfactory. Three realistic aims can be
set which we are still a long way from achieving.
Firstly, we should consider what is involved in giving
minority children the real equality of opportunity to
which Roy Jenkins refers. Here I would suggest that
without some considerable adaptation of the system to
ensure that someone not proficient in English culture
is not put at a disadvantage at the outset, there can
be no serious talk of equality of opportunity.
Secondly, we should consider the importance of
secondary cultures in our society. One does not have
to claim that minority cultures should have full
equality with that of the majority in the larger
context, in order to argue that Punjabi language,

culture and history should enjoy the same support and
respect as is accorded to French language, culture and
history in our schools; or that English culture could
be profoundly enriched through the assimilation of
elements from the minority cultures. It is also true
that cultural maintenance amongst minorities is
important for individual identity and psychological
survival, even though, if this point is taken in
isolation, it can be pressed in a patronizing, if not
a racist way. Finally, if there is an official
commitment in our society to anti-racism, that can and
should be built into the curriculum at all levels,
both in that part of the syllabus which is supposed to
deal with moral education or education for
citizenship, and through the elimination of racist
elements from textbooks and courses in other subjects.
I would suggest that serious attention given to these
points would involve concrete policies going far
beyond the present combination of highflown rhetoric
about education for a multicultural society, with ad
hoc programmes of education in English as a second
language, and patronising programmes which separate
and label minority children under the guise of
maintaining minority cultures.

Schools and Equality of Opportunity

Ideally, schools are supposed to be places in which
children of the most varied abilities are allowed to
benefit to the maximum of their capacities. On the
one hand, a minority will go on to take 'O' and 'A'
levels and some will go on to higher education; while
on the other, children not suited to these courses
will not simply waste their time, but will have their
experience enriched and their capacities improved so
that whatever jobs they do after leaving, they will
have gained the maximum from their education. The
rhetoric of a democratic society demands that whatever
the outcome in the selection process, all children and
all adults ultimately have equal value.

The sociology of education inevitably leads to a more
cynical view because it sees the schools as having a
function within a class society. It sees the
credentialling system of the schools as a means
whereby the privileges of the middle classes are
reinforced, together with a small amount of leeway for
social promotion of a few working class children.
Along with selection, it sees the school system as one

which also rejects the majority of children and implicitly prepares them for subordinate roles (Willis 1977). It also draws attention to the importance of working-class youth cultures which are anti-academic in nature, as the means whereby the rejected children preserve their identities in the face of an unjust selective system. These problems, moreover, are not seen as disappearing with comprehensivization, but as being brought more sharply into focus as the academic culture and the countercultures of the rejected children confront one another within the same institutions.

Teachers in this situation make various compromises. Most of them, being products of the selective system themselves, are drawn towards helping the maximum number of working-class children to get through the selective process, but at the same time are often profoundly uneasy about the whole credentialling process. The result is a confusion of attitudes in which an attempt is made to offer those who are rejected some kind of alternative, which too easily becomes an education for inferiority. Alternative education in a school system and a society in which the credentialling system remains, can mean simply the betrayal of those children to whom it is offered.

If these problems are acute and endemic within the system for working class children, they are much more so for the ethnic minority child. He or she faces a problem of acceptance both in relation to the valued academic culture and in terms of the counterculture of the majority culture children. We are inclined, however, to regard the system as having succeeded if the ethnic minority boy or girl either gains acceptance in mainstream working-class society, or if he or she is offered some other form of alternative education.

West Indian children face these problems in a particularly acute form. Since a number of them are successful in sports, and since the music which plays so large a part in the counterculture is one of the few genuinely multi-racial features of our culture, entry into the society and culture of working-class youth is open to them. Some, on the other hand, aware that there are strong racist elements in this society and culture which reject them, develop a counterculture of their own. From the official point of view, the Black counterculture in the form of phenomena like Rastafarianism is regarded as particularly dangerous and subversive. There is a sense of relief if a Black child becomes like any other working class child, and the schools remain systematically hostile to the Black counterculture, either seeking to eliminate it entirely, or offering it, and hence controlling it, as a part of the syllabus.

Asian parents often have a more perceptive understanding of the system. J.S. Furnivall once remarked that it was wrong to criticise Indians in India who engaged in certificate-hunting rather than seeking practical education, since, as he saw it, after many years as a colonial administrator, they were quite right in recognizing that in a society which valued certificates, particularly those leading to White Collar work, education for certificates was the most practical sort of education which there was. Not surprisingly therefore, we find that Asian parents may take a severely instrumental attitude to education. They accept the challenge of the credentialling system and try to ensure that their children get as far as they can within it. On the other hand, they accept it for what it is. They do not necessarily regard it as education in a high and valued culture, because they remain convinced that their own culture has much to commend it when compared with that of the majority population. Officially we respond to these parental attitudes by welcoming the degree to which they place value on competitive success, but seek to contain the element of a recalcitrant culture by offering it in a diluted form within the lower reaches of the system.

Central to the understanding of the way in which minority cultures are treated in the schools, is how the whole question of social and moral education is treated. Even amongst British children, education in social matters is regarded as something which is offered to the duller child who cannot cope with second and third European languages or other academic subjects. Partly we want to fill up his or her timetable. Partly we try to use these subjects for purposes of social control. Education in minority cultures fits all too easily into this educational niche. The problem facing those of us who believe that multicultural education has an important role in ensuring equality of opportunity is to see to it that it does not.

Segregation

The first issue to be faced if we are serious about providing a multicultural yet equal education to all children is that of segregation. At present, most minority children are concentrated in inner city schools where the percentage of children of West Indian and Asian ancestry is as high as 98% in some cases, and is quite commonly well above 70%. The remaining children are to be found in middle and outer-ring schools where the proportions range from about 20% to next to nothing. Unfortunately, the problems posed by this segregation have usually been seen in terms of the threat to the White children of an ethnic minority presence. Here we must ask what is likely to happen to the minority children - white and black - in these polar types of schools?

It is by no means certain that minority children who form a small minority of the population in their schools, will be better provided for than those in the more segregated schools. All too often such schools have no normal way and no resources for dealing with the special problems of minority children which are of a linguistic and cultural kind, but do have resources for dealing with remedial, backward and disciplinary cases. As a result, the Headteacher, harassed as he is with many other resource problems, may entrust the care of the minority children who have problems to the remedial teacher. Thus the minority child is more than likely to be seen as a remedial child.

This, however, is by no means to argue that all will be well in the heavily segregated school. True, it may benefit from positive discrimination, and the Headteacher will be forced to treat the problems of the minority children as the central ones in his or her school. If, however, we take the American experience seriously, we know that there is a prima facie case that segregated education is inherently unequal, and we should have to ask what actually goes on in these segregated schools. Obviously much will depend upon the special skills and sensitivities of the teachers involved. But with a low proportion of qualified teachers drawn from the minority groups, and with those who do teach having only a partial and inadequate training in either educational or multicultural problems, it must be the case that the vast majority of these schools are failing the children. One is told by teachers, "ours is essentially a remedial school", or "the school organization and curriculum are directed towards C.S.E. Mode 3" and, if these experiences are typical, it must be the case that the schools concerned are failing to offer their children anything like equality of opportunity.

What then is to be done? Ideally, the problem should be solved on the level of housing and social policy which leads to a natural process of dispersal, and in other contexts this is what I would be campaigning for. If natural dispersal were achieved one could then address oneself to the question of a multicultural policy in a normal school. But it would be utopian and a betrayal of the present generation of children to say that this was the only way in which the problem could be solved. We have therefore to consider the question of what can be done both in highly segregated schools, and in those in which West Indian and Asian children are in a minority. We need to raise the aspirations of teachers in the segregated schools so that they aim not at concentrated remedialism but at competing with the very best schools, and we need to see to it that suitable flexible resources are provided in the schools with smaller minority populations. There is even a case for arguing that it is the minority child in a dispersed situation who should be the special beneficiary of positive discrimination.

At the same time, of course, something could be done to achieve a measure of desegregation. In this area as in others forced dispersal measures like bussing are to be rejected, but much could be done to increase parental and children's choice through flexible zoning schemes. A much wider degree of choice is afforded to suburban and rural children at present than is available to inner city children, and the discrimination in this area has to be opposed as a matter of policy. Research would probably show that existing zoning schemes have had an opposite aim, namely that of containing the problems of the segregated schools and their children in the inner city.[1]

Language

Whatever the proportions of minority children in a school, our main interest should be in ensuring that each educational problem should be dealt with <u>as</u> an educational problem. Children with genuine remedial problems should be dealt with, regardless of race, as children with remedial problems. Children from broken and disturbed homes should be dealt with as children from broken and disturbed homes. Children with special linguistic and cultural problems should be dealt with as children with special linguistic and cultural problems, and so on (Rex & Moore 1967). Any multicultural policy which obscures these questions will do more harm than good. What we have to do is to develop and allocate within the system all these separate and special teaching skills. All of us are in danger of confusing the issues here as a result of the inherent racism in our culture, even if, in an educational context, this racism is of the paternalistic kind.

An appreciation of this central point should help us to understand that our very first task is to ensure that all children entering our schools are able to learn to learn, and are not totally confused, disorganised and discouraged at the moment of their entry. One has only to consider what would be involved for one's own children if they were forced to have their schooling in a foreign language and culture, in order to understand just how acute these problems are.

It is the same for an immigrant child in Britain. The point is often forcefully made in conferences like this by lecturers from minority groups beginning their lectures with five minutes of unannounced Gujerati or Spanish. The audience feels confused, and more than that, it feels that it has been subject either to some kind of gross error or a deliberate dirty trick. That is exactly how the non-English speaking child feels.

---

[1] See Secondary Allocation Sub-Committee of Reading Council of Community Relations, <u>Structural Inequality in School Allocation</u>. To be published in the <u>Journal of the National Association for Multi-cultural Education</u>, 1981.

The obvious answer is to ensure that at the outset those children who have no English should have all of their teaching in all subjects in their mother tongue. When they have gained confidence in this way it is then possible for them to be gradually transferred to instruction in English, via English as a second language classes, as they develop the kind of English which is appropriate to the kinds of study they are called upon to do. In urging the systematic adoption of a mother tongue programme, I am fully aware of the difficulties. I am also aware of the view conscientiously held by some, that it is best simply to throw children in at the deep end. But the case for mother tongue instruction has hardly been considered in this country. We need to look at the experience of countries like Sweden, where at least for the more concentrated minorities like the Finns, it is widely accepted that the children are receiving less than their proper and normal social rights if nothing is done to take account of their special problems. Obviously, there is a huge problem of finding and appropriately allocating resources here, but it is astonishing that even after entering the E.E.C. we have done so little even to begin to deal with these problems.

We have of course done more, at least in some LEAs, to provide for instruction in English as a second language. But here again the situation is far from perfect. Our goal should be firstly to ensure that at the appropriate point in the curriculum, children are introduced to English either in the course of the normal syllabus or in special withdrawal classes. We then have to ensure that, if they have been withdrawn, they are not reinserted into the system in a way in which they cannot be expected to cope. They cannot sensibly be expected to catch up with a huge backlog of work in which the native-born children have gone ahead of them. Then they must go on improving their English so that they have it sufficiently in their command not to be held back in achieving the highest level of educational success of which they would otherwise be capable.

Biculturalism

Related to the problem of language is the question of biculturalism. Prima facie it would seem to be the case that a child who comes into school from a home where an entirely different culture survives, will have problems on the cultural and not only on the linguistic level. He or she should, therefore, be given the opportunity in school of continuing to learn about and explore the possibilities of that culture. Such a minority culture education programme would appear to be necessary if the child is not to lose all sense of identity, or come to believe that his home culture is inferior or lacking in legitimacy.

Having said this, I should immediately go on to say that there are many who would assent to what has been said without fully understanding what it means. Multicultural education provided in a paternalistic way to all children who happen to have black skins, without serious consideration of what the needs of each specific child are, could have the effect of simply labelling black children as inferior. The way to avoid this is by associating the parents and the minority communities as closely as possible with these programmes. Of particular importance here is home-school liaison, and a serious attempt to bring together what is done in supplementary schools and what is done within the school itself. Equally important is the employment of minority teachers who are capable of teaching their own culture; but, and this is esential, who also enjoy respect because they are members of subject departments and teach other subjects.

One problem which must be faced squarely here is that our natural inclination is to see minority cultures as both alien and dangerous, and as subversive. This is particularly true so far as the West Indian community is concerned. Obviously, we are told, we cannot have people teaching the extreme forms of Rastafarianism in our schools. I think that that is true. But the problem which we face here is not an entirely new one. We always have been a bicultural and a class divided society. Workingclass culture with its strong socialist elements has been seen as subversive of the individualistic, achievement-oriented culture within a class context. But this is also a liberal and democratic society, and over the years we have evolved, at least in our better schools, ways of teaching social history and related subjects in a manner which does justice to working class values. What is wanted in relation to education in minority cultures is neither a paternalistic and watered down version of the culture used primarily to achieve social control, nor political propaganda more appropriate to directly political situations, but rather an acceptance of the cultural and educational importance of the minority cultures, akin to that which has been partially accorded to the sophisticated political culture of the British working classes.

Education in minority cultures will always be regarded as nothing more than a paternalistically conceded sop, however, so long as it is confined to what Jennifer Williams (1979) has referred to as the low-status uncertificated parts of the curriculum. The question therefore is how far we can include it in the high-status certificated parts of the curriculum. Why not, that is to say, have Punjabi, Gujerati, Urdu, Indian or Pakistani culture and history, Caribbean culture and history, African history and other such subjects available for study up to the highest level?

The problem here does not lie with the Examining Boards. Most of these subjects probably can be taken for 'O' and 'A' level examinations. The problem lies with the schools and their disposition of resources. It will be argued that we cannot have an infinite number of new subjects taught. But surely there would be demand for these. We do not have a million French settlers in this country, but we encourage children to study French language, literature and history. We certainly do not have many Romans and Greeks here, but we go on providing Classics. Why not then teach the cultures and languages and histories of the minority populations in a serious scholarly way, both the living traditions and their classical equivalents? (I have heard it suggested, for example that able Pakistani students might like to take Arabic as an 'O' and 'A' level subject).

All this does not mean that we are going to become a multicultural society in which the minority cultures have a politically guaranteed equal status. It does mean though that we will take these cultures seriously as secondary cultures in Britain, and as having a prestigious and not an inferior status in their own right. This would be important for race relations generally, and it might also ensure that the multicultural element lower down the school curriculum was taken seriously.

A Multicultural Curriculum

Finally, under the general heading of an 'ideal-but-realistic' policy on multicultural education, I should like to consider what should be done as a result of the development of such a policy for the white British child. Clearly one thing which might be offered is the option of studying the minorities' culture, history and language at a high level. If this were brought within the credentialling system the British child would have every incentive to take an interest. What would not be of any great value would be lectures pitched at a moralistic, 'Sunday-school' level, divorced from the study of subjects which have a credentialling pay-off.

Another somewhat rhetorical suggestion which is sometimes made about the education of the majority-culture child is that the whole content of the school curriculum and of school text-books needs to be rewritten to prepare him for membership of a multicultural society. Of course this is of importance, but if it is not to be a matter of rhetoric only, what we need to be doing is considering what practical steps have to be taken. To what extent have existing examination schemes to be altered? Are there specific curriculum projects which we should be asking for, either to modify existing subjects or to propose new ones? Apparently, Little and Willey (1981) found that there is no opposition to changes of these kinds from the examining boards. There has simply been no demand for them from teachers, parents or anyone else. But in any case, the English educational system is a very open one. The problem for those who believe in multiculturalism and anti-racism is to get down to writing better books, and devising better courses, in the full knowledge that others with more traditional and racist ideas will also be busy writing theirs.

Related to this is the question of specific teaching against racism. Stenhouse's (1979) research in this area seems to suggest that some of the strategies which might be pursued will be at best negative in their effects and at worst counter-productive. But this, of course, relates to anti-racism taken in isolation. There does seem to be considerable scope for anti-racist education within the broader context of social and political studies. The problem here turns first on how far we do in fact ensure that social and political education becomes a part of the normal curriculum at all levels, and secondly on how an anti-racist element can be written into the curriculum. One would have thought that the latter could be done since our society is at least formally committed to anti-racism. What has to be avoided is a situation in which a particular teacher is left to evangelise against racism either on a moralistic or a political basis. The anti-racist theme has to appear in formal and public syllabuses.

It may be said here that by focussing attention too much on the higher reaches of the curriculum, I am ignoring the fact that the real locus of racism in the school will be found amongst the young 'skinheads' and others who will never take C.S.Es let alone 'O' and 'A' levels. This may be so, but I do not think we can resolve the problem merely by preaching at skinheads. Their very existence is a sign of the failure of the middle class credentialling culture of the normal school, and of traditional and politically sophisticated working class culture. It is a problem which has to be tackled both by improved education in the schools and by political struggle outside. A multi-racial and anti-racist society has to be fought for simultaneously on many fronts. Perhaps it is worth noting that the issue has been joined already within the working class counter-cultures. Some of these at least are already committed to anti-racism.

A Critique of Present Policies

In the above sections I have suggested that a serious approach to multicultural education which is at once ideal and realistic should take account of:

1. The problems engendered by segregation and dispersal of ethnic minority children
2. The problem of mother tongue instruction
3. The problem of teaching English as a 'second language' in ways which maximise educational opportunity
4. The problem of the teaching of minority cultures at lower levels, in ways which increase educational opportunity rather than labelling and segregating minority children
5. The problem of introducing subjects related to minority cultures at higher levels and within the credentialling system of our schools
6. The problem of political education of white British children for an anti-racist society.

I have suggested that these are all the problems which need to be solved by the development of appropriate skills and techniques. They are the problems to which teacher education should address itself.

Against this background we can proceed to judge the actual policies which have been developed under the title 'multi-cultural education', and the political concerns which lie behind them.

Significantly, the first response on an official level to the presence of ethnic minority children in schools was that they were the problem. Even Lord Boyle, who in so many other respects played an important part in the developing of an anti-racist position within the Conservative Party, responded to the arrival of large numbers of immigrant children in schools with the idea that a percentage of 30% immigrant children in schools was too high, and this belief led to proposals for bussing. Sadly, this idea, which, in America, had been part of a programme to increase the rights of the black child in the educational system and in the wider society, was adopted in England in a perverse way, with the sole emphasis being on the thinning out of blacks lest they should adversely affect the education of the English child. When bussing was abandoned and inner city schools became even more sharply segregated, the interest in the dangers of segregation died out completely.

The overwhelming concern of our multicultural policies has been with English as a second language, conceived not as a problem for the child so much as a problem for the schools. Just as black children had to be moved to ensure the continued effective education of white British children, so also foreign languages had to be removed lest they prevent normal teaching. Moreover, since the aim of E.S.L. teaching was not to ensure equality of opportunity, attention was focussed solely on equipping children with elementary English to enable them to just survive in a classroom situation, with little concern if any for enabling those who had been withdrawn from normal courses to catch up. The programme has been consistent with enabling the majority of children to cope minimally with school work and then go on to unskilled industrial jobs. If many Asian children survived this process and actually achieved educational success, it was despite the programmes rather than because of them.

We have also dwelt ad nauseam on the failure rate
amongst West Indian children, but have coupled this
with the repeated diagnosis that it is due to
something called 'disadvantage'. Instead of providing
a special centre for the development of appropriate
resources to help ethnic minority children, we created
a Centre on Educational Disadvantage. The specific
and particular problems of the minority child were
therefore merged and confused at the highest policy
level, as they were also in the schools with a wide
range of categories of other children who were
troublesome.

Against that background, the energies of good and
morally committed teachers were mobilised to provide a
very limited multicultural curriculum provided in a
paternalistic if not in a damning way. Little if
anything has been done to provide education in
minority cultures at a higher level, and consequently
such programmes as existed at lower levels have always
been lacking in status and legitimacy. Finally, we
have not been able to develop any serious programmes
for white British children which would encourage
respect for minority children or have the effect of
reducing racism. Political education as a part of the
core curriculum gives way to a mushy amalgam of
Christianity and middle class morality.

Agents of Change

The emphasis of this paper has been on realistic
goals, rather than rhetoric. We have to admit that in
our society as it is, there will be overwhelming
pressure to use multicultural education like any other
form of education, to prepare the majority of ethnic
minority children for their role as members of an
underclass. But to be a realist is not to be a
fatalist. There are many in education from the highest
policy making levels downwards who do not see
themselves as agents for the perpetuation of the
status quo. They will campaign and they will argue,
and it is to them above all that this paper is
addressed. The question is not one of what the
Department of Education and Science or the Local
Education Authorities will provide. It is what policy
makers and teachers who share a commitment to an equal
and anti-racist society will decide to do in terms of
their shared beliefs. No one will be more crucial in
this process than those who are responsible in
Colleges, Polytechnics and Universities for the
training of teachers.

REFERENCES

Commonwealth Immigrants Advisory Council (1964), 2nd Report (Cmnd. 2266), H.M.S.O.

Little, A. & Willey, R. (1981), _Multi-ethnic Education: the way forward_, The Schools Council

Patterson, S. (1969), _Immigration and Race Relations in Britain 1960-1967_, Oxford University Press

Rex, J. & Moore, R. (1967), _Race, Community and Conflict_, Oxford University Press

Secondary Allocation Sub-Committee of the Reading Council of Community Relations (1980), "Structural inequality in school allocation", in _Multiracial Education_, Vol. 9, No. 1

Stenhouse, L. (1979), "Problems and effects of teaching about race relations", in _The Social Science Teacher_, Vol. 8, No. 4

Williams, J. (1979), "Perspectives on the multicultural curriculum", in _The Social Science Teacher_, Vol. 8, No. 4

Willis, P. (1977), _Learning to Labour_, Saxon House

DISCUSSION

The most significant points raised in discussion are listed below. The discussion was mostly concerned with the more specific policy objectives considered by Professor Rex, but some time was devoted at the outset to the broader aims of multicultural education.

1. ### Pluralism vs. social cohesion

   If the aims of multicultural education are to include the celebration of cultural diversity (as contrasted with the assimilation of ethnic minorities to the majority culture), are there limits to this? Is there not a tension between the twin societal aims of cultural pluralism and social cohesion? If the former takes precedence, the educational implications appear to take us in the direction of separate schooling, social segregation, and perhaps increased social conflict. Is the problem in a social democracy to contain both aims in a delicate balance?

2. ### Special needs vs. multicultural education for all pupils

   The distinction between equipping teachers to meet the special needs of ethnic minority children (e.g. in respect of English as a second language), and of preparing them to help all children towards a fuller appreciation of life in a multicultural society, was brought out repeatedly throughout the seminar. Both objectives were felt to be important, neither should be neglected. But it was thought that teacher educators, and perhaps more significantly, course validators, (i.e. CNAA and Universities), were not always fully aware of both objectives: they tended towards a special needs approach.

3. ### Mother Tongue teaching

   Teaching through the mother tongue for young children starting school can signal that the home language is valued and respected. This may enhance home-school relations, and can be of benefit to the pupil's personal development as well as to his/her education. As to longer-term objectives, competence in English is fundamental to maintaining a wide range of opportunities for

young people in British society, and all therefore
need to acquire this competence. A bicultural
policy in schools, however, would also allow
ethnic minority children to maintain their mother
tongue and culture.

4. Culture maintenance

Mother tongue teaching and the study of mother
culture in schools might be of great value in
helping to sustain cultural continuity between
ethnic minority pupils and their parents, and in
contributing to a more positive feeling of
identity for such pupils in an alienating world.
However, it is important to allow for choice, for
some pupils (and their parents) may prefer to
assimilate and not to maintain their home language
or culture. Whichever the choice, the school's
primary aim should be to provide all pupils with
access to the majority culture.

5. Race relations teaching

In addition to preparing teachers to meet the
special needs of ethnic minority children, and to
sensitising them to use with all children
appropriate books and materials in a non-
ethnocentric curriculum, there is a need for a
third element: some knowledge of the area of race
relations teaching. Attempts need to be made to
enable teachers to consider intercultural
stereotyping, prejudice and racism, perhaps
through those areas of the curriculum concerned
with moral, social or political education.

Chapter Three

THE RESEARCH CONTEXT

Sally Tomlinson

Beginning with a review of research relating to teacher expectations in multicultural classrooms, Dr Tomlinson goes on to consider aspects of curriculum and organisation, and the implications for teacher education.

"Quote from a Midlands staff room: 'We've had mixed ability; we've gone community, and now its bloody multiculturalism'." (Birley High School 1980).

A.H. Halsey pointed out in 1972 that too much has been claimed for the power of education systems to act as instruments of wholesale reform, in societies which are hierarchical in their distribution of life-chances between races, classes and sexes. He might also have noted that too much has been claimed of teachers in such societies to act as instruments of social change via educational innovation. The National Union of Teachers, in an early statement concerning the education of the children of immigrants,[1] showed itself to be very much aware of the contradictions inherent in the teacher's role in a multicultural society.

> ⌐Education⌐ ... "is at one and the same time the instrument for the maintenance of an ordered society and the preservation of its accepted ethos ... and for the continuation of its chosen way of life, and yet it must serve as an agency for social change." (N.U.T. 1967).

The N.U.T. advised its members to "fearlessly work out solutions" to problems of cultural and racial diversity despite "disapprobation from some groups" or "unmerited applause" from others. However, the quote from a Midlands staffroom at the beginning of this paper possibly encapsulates the frustration which many

---

[1] In their 1967 statement on <u>The Education of Immigrants</u>, the N.U.T. described the education of these children as "one of the most critical problems in education today."

teachers have felt when fearless educational
innovation and change are demanded of them, within
wider social and political constraints and divisions
which they are unable to control.

This paper takes a sympathetic view of the position of
teachers, who perhaps too often, have been the objects
of research and exhortation concerning their job in a
multicultural society, rather than receiving much
actual assistance in preparation for, or in doing,
that job. Teachers have provided easy targets for
critical attack, without sufficient attempts having
been made to locate them, historically or culturally,
within the contradictions of a society which offers
both a rhetoric concerning multiracial, multicultural
harmony, and a reality of pragmatic intolerance and
hostility. The paper is concerned to provide a review
of research pertaining to teachers and teacher
education in a multicultural society, and to point to
areas where a need for research information might lie.
It will therefore have the following objectives:

1. To describe some of the research on teacher
   expectations, attitudes and opinions
   concerning minority group children, and the
   links made between expectations, attitudes
   and poor pupil performance.

2. To discuss research on teacher perceptions
   about school organization, language,
   curriculum and curriculum change for a
   multicultural society.

3. To briefly examine research and comment on
   teacher education and training.

4. To note the paucity of research information on
   the employment and careers of minority group
   teachers.

Finally, the paper indicates that a major need and
opportunity in the 1980s is not so much to do research
on teachers, but rather with teachers, to prevent
polarisation and antagonism between researchers and
practitioners.

Expectations, Attitudes and Opinions

Research indicating the importance of teacher

expectations and attitudes on the subsequent academic and behavioural performance of all children began to filter through to teachers and teacher trainers by the late 1960s. The publication of Rosenthal and Jacobson's <u>Pygmalion in the Classroom</u> (1968) in the U.S.A., and the work of Pidgeon and Yates at the N.F.E.R. (Pidgeon 1970) indicated a complex relationship between teacher expectations, pupil reaction to teacher expectations, and their conformity to these expectations in terms of academic performance and behaviour. Bernard Coard's influential polemic (1972) used Rosenthal and Jacobson's work to support his contention that teacher expectations and attitudes towards black children caused them to seriously underestimate the ability of black children.

"Most teachers absorb the brainwashing that everybody else in the society has absorbed - that black people are inferior, less intelligent, than whites." (<u>Op.cit</u>. 1972)

However, Rist's (1970) work in the U.S.A. demonstrated a link between teacher expectations of some black children and their subsequent poorer performance even where the teacher was herself black.

A major problem in research which links teacher expectations, attitudes and opinions with poorer academic performance is that the links are difficult to provide empirically; they are largely logical. Thus, it is logical to assume that if teachers hold stereotyped opinions and expectations of black children, this may lead to different teaching techniques and classroom treatment which works to the detriment of the children's education. There is a small but significant amount of research indicating that teachers do hold stereotyped views about minority group children, particularly West Indian children, and that their views may be linked to poorer academic performance and behaviour.

The most comprehensive survey of teacher opinion to date was that undertaken by Elaine Brittan as the third phase of the D.E.S.-sponsored N.F.E.R. study, begun in 1970 (Townsend 1971; Townsend and Brittan 1972). Brittan obtained postal questionnaire data from 510 teachers at 171 primary schools, and 339 teachers at 25 secondary schools in 1972, asking 40 questions "appraising teachers' professional opinions on aspects of life in multiracial schools." In an

article discussing teacher opinion of their pupils in
schools with both high and low concentrations of
minority group children (Brittan 1976), she noted the
willingness of teachers to make generalisations about
children of West Indian origin and to produce
contradictory stereotypes, (black pupils described as
lazy/passive/withdrawn, and also as boisterous/
aggressive/disruptive), which they were not willing to
make about white or Asian children. She pointed out
that "it is clear that teachers perceive West Indian
pupils as of low ability and as creating discipline
problems." (Op.cit. 1976)

Brittan was the evaluator for a further piece of
research on education for a multiracial society,
sponsored by the Schools Council and carried out at
the N.F.E.R. from 1973-76, she and Townsend having
carried out a preliminary survey for this project
during 1972-73 (Townsend and Brittan 1973). It was
this research which resulted in some controversy when
the Schools Council decided not to publish the report
of the project, (see letters to The Times Educational
Supplement, 10 and 24 Feb. 1978 and 10 Mar. 1978). The
first draft chapter of this project was published in
New Society (16 Feb. 1978), and it appeared that the
research seemed to support the contention that
teachers' opinions and perceptions of children of
different race were inappropriate. In particular, "the
childrens' comments largely contradict what the
teachers have to say." The suggestion was that the
teachers' own (ethnocentric) education, experiences,
and lack of information about minority groups leads
them to make inappropriate assumptions about the
children. These assumptions were compounded by the way
race is presented solely as a problem in British
society, and the reluctance of minority children to
"present their real selves in school."

Giles, who had been a visiting fellow at the N.F.E.R.
on the 'Education for a multiracial society' project,
produced a book in 1977 on The West Indian Experience
in British Schools. Part of that experience, he
concluded, had to do with the way "teacher stereotypes
and teacher expectations do influence the way they
behave towards West Indian students, and have an
influence on the interaction process." Giles visited
23 multiracial schools in Inner London, 15 infant and
8 secondary, and on the basis of interviews and
observation he became "convinced that there are both
subtle and overt forms of discrimination taking place

in British schools, resulting from teachers' attitudes and behaviour ... towards West Indian students." (Op.cit. 1977)

Driver, in his study in the early 1970s of a Handworth secondary school, (Driver 1977, 1979) also pointed to cultural incongruities which are responsible for teacher difficulties in making judgments about the ability and behaviour of West Indian pupils. Cultural misconceptions could lead to West Indin pupils "being vulnerable to poor assessment of their abilities." (Op.cit. 1979) Driver pointed to a variety of ways in which cultural misunderstandings could arise, which resulted in teachers feeling threatened and anxious in their dealings with West Indian pupils.

In a study of referral into ESN(M) education in the mid-1970s, Tomlinson (1981) came to conclusions similar to those of Brittan, Giles, and Driver after interviews with 30 headteachers and some 20 class teachers. As far as West Indian pupils were concerned, it did seem that "teachers tend to operate within a framework of stereotypes, which are reinforced rather than negated, by pupil response," (Op.cit.) The teachers produced contradictory stereotypes: the West Indian pupils were "a representative bunch, slow, docile and low functioning", and "the usual problem – hyperactive and anti-authority." Some teachers felt threatened by the behaviour of their adolescent West Indian pupils, linking this to the militant black response to white society. "We are a black power area, and it is very dangerous; the black power people destroy kids, particularly the less able."

Edwards (1978, 1979) has provided further evidence of a logical connection between teachers' cultural assumptions and the poorer academic performance of West Indian children. Her work with 20 student teachers showed that they evaluated West Indian dialect speech lower than working class speech even when spoken by the same girl, and that "speech types serve as identifiers which evoke stereotypes held by ourselves and others." (Op.cit. 1979)

This kind of research does suggest that teachers' own cultural beliefs and assumptions, and their lack of knowledge of minority group cultures may affect teacher behaviour - via attitude and expectation - in the classroom. They may teach in ways that produce

lower academic achievement, or react in defensive ways
to disruptive black pupils. Little and Willey (1981)
in their recent study, replicating Townsend and
Brittan's earlier national survey of L.E.A.s, found
that "many authorities and schools emphasised the
importance of teacher attitudes, both in terms of
helping the teacher to develop positive attitudes to
cultural diversity, and convincing them that they
should consider the implications of a multi-ethnic
society for their teaching."

However, Stone (1981) takes issue with research which
suggests that teachers should acquire knowledge of the
cultural background of black children and should
change their attitudes to improve black self-concept
and self-esteem, (e.g. Bagley & Coard 1975). In her
research in three London schools which placed an
emphasis on multiracial education, with three
comparison schools and with four community
project/supplementary schools, she concluded that
teachers who stress self-concept and self-esteem did
so at the expense of concrete educational objectives.
"The practical result of these assumptions is that
teachers act more and more like social workers, and
consequently neglect their primary role of
instruction." (Op.cit.)

Research on teacher attitudes, and action based on the
assumption that teacher attitudes need changing is
currently under attack from two directions. One, a
direction indicated by Stone, representing a black
viewpoint; and the second, a direction indicated by
Hastie (1981) who argues that multicultural
enthusiasts may divide and antagonise teachers rather
than 'consolidate racial harmony'.

Organisation, Language, Curriculum and Curriculum Change

While attitudes and expectations are nebulous
characteristics which are not easily amenable to
change, school organisation and curriculum are more
tangible and changeable. Research into teachers' views
about multiracial school organisation, about language
needs, and about developing multicultural education
would seem relevant and necessary. Also, as Stenhouse
noted in 1975, "Although there is a clear need to
prepare pupils for life in a multiracial society, and
a good many schools and teachers are working on the
problems, there is a shortage of research to support
them". (Op.cit.)

Townsend and Brittan's (1972) research was the first
national survey of organisation in multiracial
schools. A postal questionnaire to 132 primary and 98
secondary schools provided information on the teaching
of English, the assessment of ability, grouping and
streaming, staffing, home-school liaison and other
topics. They concluded that "there has been a constant
adaptation of tried and tested procedures to untried
and untested circumstances which speaks volumes for
the flexibility of teachers in England." (Op.cit.)
However, much of the adaptation did consist of
arrangements to teach ESL; as Townsend and Brittan put
it, "It is apparent that the teaching of English to
non-English speaking pupils is seen by multiracial
schools as their major task." (Op.cit.)

Schools have continued to conceptualise their major
multicultural task as that of teaching ESL at both
'first' and 'second' phase, and Derrick's Language
Needs of Minority Children (1977) provides a
comprehensive description of research and curriculum
projects, aimed at understanding different language
needs and organising to satisfy these needs. Derrick
noted that the language needs of West Indian children
were neglected, and the 'Bullock Report', A Language
for Life (1975) made a strong plea for more research
to help West Indian children with language, but apart
from Edwards' work (1979) there has been little
response. ESL teaching fitted in well with the
assimilationist ideology of the 1960s (Bolton 1979),
but with the adoption of models of cultural pluralism
the issues of bilingual learning and mother-tongue
teaching became important. Derrick (1977) pointed to
the 1967 Bilingual Education Act in the U.S.A. which
allowed for the early education of minority group
children in their own mother tongue, but bilingualism
has not become a major theme in British research or
practice.

Similarly, the extent of demand for and provision of
mother tongue teaching in Britain is unclear, although
Khan's 'Linguistic Minorities Project' (1979-82) will
shortly provide more information in this area. Little
and Willey (1981) have reported that teachers, schools
and L.E.A.s still do conceptualise their main task in
schools attended by minority group children, as
satisfying language needs. They note that 80% of
headteachers in schools with a high concentration of
Asian children were worried that 'second-phase'
English was inadequate to encourage academic

achievement, and 70% of heads were worried about the language needs of West Indian pupils. 14 L.E.A.s reported support for mother tongue teaching, but overall "there had been only a limited increase in the teaching of these languages (Urdu, Gujerati, etc) since Townsend and Brittan's report". (Op.cit.)

Teaching and research approaches to curriculum change in schools appear to fall roughly into three categories, the "teaching race relations" approach, the "insertion" approach, and the "permeation" approach. The "teaching race relations" approach, i.e. actually teaching about 'race', was perceived as an answer to "prejudice" during the 1960s. The Schools Council's 'Humanities Curriculum Project' was asked to take race relations as one of a number of topics, and to explore how to "educate for the elimination of racial tension and ill-feeling in our society, which is and always will be multiracial, by undermining prejudice, developing respect for varied traditions, and by encouraging mutual understanding, reasonableness and justice." (Stenhouse 1975). The difficulties of achieving these aims via teaching have been documented by Harmingson (1973), Parkinson and MacDonald (1972) and Stenhouse (1975). Further research into direct teaching about race has not been forthcoming, but there are some indications that teachers feel a need for actual curriculum materials to combat racism,[2] particularly since the recent re-emergence of extreme right-wing movements in schools (see Vennig 1981).

The conceptualisation of "black studies" courses as a means by which teachers could show that they valued minority group pupils and their cultures, spread, as Giles (1976) noted, from intellectuals, teachers and community workers downwards; whereas in America, demand had spread "from the streets to the Universities." The variety of topics, both non-examinable and examinable at CSE or 'O' level, which developed under the "black studies" label in the early

---

2   See Lister (1981). I have also recently received letters from individual teachers expressing anxiety about racism in their schools, and requesting help via curriculum materials.

1970s, and the multiracial (or cultural or ethnic) label in the later 1970s, and which can loosely be described as additions or insertions to the curriculum, have not been systematically researched or evaluated. However, it is important to stress that it is largely teachers themselves who, in the absence of direction or training, have devised courses, materials and methods, and there is descriptive evidence on how some of these have developed. McNeal and Rogers' book, The Multiracial School (1971), documented teachers devising their own strategies for multiracial classes; and Townsend and Brittan (1973) included an appendix of "examples of work in a multiracial society", (some examples being the 'Black studies' course at Tulse Hill School presented by Mr. Woodroffe, 'Multi-racial history' from Mr. George at Denbigh High School, and 'Religion in a multi-faith school' from Mr. Cole at James Graham College). Cross, Baker and Styles (1977) have explored ways of helping teachers to present minority cultures in a positive manner, and the N.U.T. has produced a pamphlet, Guidelines for Teachers on Racial Stereotyping in Textbooks and Learning Materials, (N.U.T., 1979).

By the mid-1970s, emphasis had moved from the idea of inserting additions to the curriculum, to the notion of "permeation" of the whole curriculum with a multi-ethnic input. This approach has been strongly urged by Jeffcoate (1979 (a)) who has been critical of the notion that multicultural education, particularly that along insertion lines, will instil "respect" for other cultures and a consequent improvement in race relations, (1979 (b)). Little and Willey (1981) noted that a majority of all the schools they obtained information from, both with and without high concentrations of minority group children, reported discussing at meetings an "across the curriculum approach". The problem of examination relevance has been raised by James (1979), Little and Willey (1981), and Stone (1981), as the "hiving-off" of minority children into non-examinable multicultural courses came to be perceived as being at odds with the acquisition of credentials via traditional subject areas.

Research into teacher opinion on curriculum change for a multiracial, multicultural society is limited, and again Townsend and Brittan's work has provided a major source of information. Their 1972-73 survey investigated headteachers' views as to the need for curriculum development, and documented syllabuses and curriculum innovation. 435 schools in both multiracial and non-multiracial areas, both primary and secondary, completed a questionnaire, and overall "there appeared to be a considerable majority of headteachers, in all types of school, whether multiracial or not ... who consider that one of their aims should be to prepare pupils for life in a multiracial society," (Townsend & Brittan 1973). However, there was some confusion and lack of direction in achieving this aim via curriculum development. Brittan's (1976) study of 510 teachers included questions on curriculum and school organisation, and she concluded that "there is little evidence of the schools ... effecting curricular changes or even a high level of awareness of the needs." She found that a majority of teachers believed 'assimilation' to be the aim of a multiracial society, and they thus tended to stress English language teaching but little else.

While systematic research is lacking, there is evidence that many schools and teachers are continuing to take the initiative in producing courses and curriculum materials, and even attempting to 'permeate' the whole curriculum, (Birley High School 1980). Publishers are also becoming aware of the need to help teachers by producing books suitable for a multicultural curriculum, (Klein 1981). However, the need for systematic research on what has begun to take place in the area of curriculum development, to evaluate its success, and to encourage development both in multiracial areas and in 'white' areas, would seem to be paramount.

Teacher Education

It will be apparent that research during the past fifteen years has provided us with some information about how teachers have perceived their pupils and their tasks, since the schools and the society in which they work became multiracial and multicultural. However, it is important to stress that teacher attitudes, opinions and expectations of minority group children, and their willingness and ability to make curriculum changes depends in a large part on the preparation and help they have received through teacher training courses. It is also important to note that the teachers who have been the subjects of research to date, have largely been the products of an inadequate training. If teachers do demonstrate inappropriate attitudes, or lack knowledge about their minority group pupils or about the most appropriate ways of teaching in a multicultural society, teacher training must bear some of the blame.

A brief examination of the history of teacher training for a multicultural society does demonstrate that the task of proper teacher preparation for what has been, in effect, a momentous change in the composition of the school population, has never been regarded as an urgent priority. E.J.B. Rose, in 1969, was able to document developments which had taken place up to that date. He noted that Ann Blatch, a former Huddersfield teacher, pioneered a one-term in-service course in English as a second language at the London Institute of Education, and that the early training of teachers was oriented towards language courses. By the late 1960s, some Colleges of Education had begun to provide optional courses on the "Teaching of immigrant children" and "Education for a multicultural society", a pioneer being Edge Hill College. But the burden of teacher training was placed on the ability and willingness of individual college staff to run courses, or on L.E.A.s to provide in-service courses. Rose wrote that during the 1960s, "the hesitant development of in-service training seems to indicate the absence of any concerted drive by the D.E.S. to get courses set up and attended." (Op.cit 1969). He particularly blamed the D.E.S. for a lack of leadership in a situation where there was an urgent need for pre-service and in-service courses. However, the D.E.S. Education Survey 13 (1971) produced a more optimistic picture of the number of colleges offering teacher training courses, although they did acknowledge that "information about the nature and extent of in-service training in the education of immigrants is far from complete." As Rose noted:

> "In 1967 it was not impossible for a teacher to find herself, without warning or preparation, in charge of a class of 40 infant children of immigrants." (Op.cit)

It is not impossible in 1981 for this situation to occur!

The early 1970s was perhaps more a period of exhortation and reiteration of the need to prepare teachers for teaching in a multiracial society, rather than of provision of courses. The 'James Report' (1972) urged that an understanding of the multicultural nature of our society should figure in all teacher training. The Select Committee on Race and Immigration in 1973 considered that in-service training was more important than initial training, and that existing in-service courses were inadequate. The Committee also noted that "all students on initial or postgraduate courses can and should be aware that wherever they teach they will be doing so in a multicultural society." The CRC/ATCDE Report, first published in 1974, contained 13 timely recommendations on teacher training, and stressed the urgency of the "challenge presented by the recent emergence of a society which contains the seeds of racial disharmony"; and the 1977 D.E.S. green paper, Education in Schools, questioned "whether existing courses of teacher education give enough attention to the role of teachers in a multicultural society."

Systematic research, and the evaluation of courses that have developed particularly during the later 1970s, is now beginning to take place; but it is worth noting that Little and Willey's recent research found that L.E.A.s providing in-service courses felt they were preaching to the converted, and that they reached only those teachers who were already convinced of the need to educate themselves in strategies and techniques for teaching in a multicultural society (Op.cit. 1981).

Ethnic Minority Teachers

Research concerning the employment and careers of ethnic minority teachers in Britain is almost completely lacking, but there is a rhetoric that the employment of such teachers would be advantageous to schools. The Select Committee on Race and Immigration in its 1973 report admitted that, "although like the D.E.S., we do not know the number of immigrant teachers employed we do know that it is not proportionate to the immigrant population," (Op.cit. 1973). But they agreed with their witnesses, which included representatives of L.E.A.s, that there ought to be more ethnic minority teachers employed "with all the advantages of understanding they would bring." The CRC/ATCDE (1974) report recommended that "colleges should give positive consideration to recruiting tutors and students from minority groups."

A small, recent research which involved the interviewing of 27 West Indian teachers, estimated that there were around 800 'black' teachers, and that the Caribbean Teachers Association know of approximately 300, (Gibbes 1980). This study indicated that West Indian teachers experienced difficulties within the British school system. They had stressful experiences in obtaining and keeping jobs, and some felt discriminated against in job promotion. They felt they had a significant contribution to make towards motivating black children to do well in school, but that failure to obtain promotion to higher positions led to low morale and to quitting the profession. A recently formed Society of Immigrant Teachers has also documented discrimination during training and probation and in promotion. The Society is reported to have asked the D.E.S. to undertake a public inquiry into the "under-achievement" of black teachers," (Lister 1980).

Needs and Opportunities

In a recent provocative publication, Stone (1981) has suggested that courses designed to prepare teachers for a multicultural society, particularly those stressing knowledge of other cultures, are unnecessary. She quotes a black teacher as saying that "the perfect teacher for West Indian children is a traditional no-nonsense teacher who knows her subject and knows how to teach." Many might feel that there is a need for specific teacher preparation for a multicultural society, so as to help the good no-nonsense teacher to teach even better. But Stones' work is timely because it may make us consider again what are the aims of teacher education for a multicultural society. It seems to me that a basic need, shared by teachers and researchers, is to clarify what we mean by a multicultural society, what the aims of teaching in this society are or should be, and how to go about teaching more effectively to achieve these aims.

It also seems to me that there is a need for any future research concerning teacher education, or teaching in a multicultural society, to be done as far as possible with, by, or in close co-operation with, teachers. It has already been noted that teachers have so far been the objects of research and exhortation, and they might justifiably begin now to reject their scapegoat label. There would seem to be <u>no</u> need for further research on teacher attitude and opinions. There might justifiably be a need for more 'factual' information about teachers and intending teachers, documenting for example the professional characteristics and actual knowledge about ethnic minority groups, of teachers in multiracial schools. This kind of research could be done by or with teachers.

The area where there would seem to be a crucial need for research is the area of curriculum development (which pre-supposes a clarification of aims for teaching in a multiracial society). As Jeffcoate (1979 b) has written:

> "In the next decade we need to hear rather more from teachers and classroom researchers about what happens, and what makes for success, when classroom and school innovations are initiated and implemented."

It is presumably the in-service training programmes which "need" research and development ideas most urgently, to fulfil the needs currently being articulated by serving teachers.

A further need would appear to be an urgent review of the employment of, and position of, ethnic minority teachers. If we are serious in seeking to provide equality of opportunity for all children in our society, we should presumably be equally serious in providing equality of opportunity for all intending teachers.

Despite the economic climate, there are opportunities to undertake research and development work concerned with teaching and teacher preparation for a multicultural society. If equality of opportunity is to be an aim in our society, teachers and researchers can work together to achieve it.

REFERENCES

Bagley. C & Coard, B. (1975), "Cultural knowledge and rejection of ethnic identity in West Indian children in London," in (eds) Bagley, C. & Verma, G. Race and Education Across Cultures, Heinemann

Birley High School (1980), Multicultural Education in the 1980s, Manchester

Bolton, E. (1979), "Education in a multiracial society," Trends in Education, 4

Brittan, E. (1976), "Teacher opinions on aspects of school life - changes in curriculum and school organisation," Educational Research, Vol. 18, No. 2

Brittan, E. (1976), "Teacher opinion on aspects of school life - pupils and teachers," Educational Research, Vol. 18, No. 3

'Bullock Report' (1975), A Language for Life, H.M.S.O.

Coard, B. (1972), How the West Indian Child is made ESN in the British School System, New Beacon Books

Cross, D., Baker, G. & Stiles, L. (1977), Teaching in a Multicultural Society - Perspectives and Professional Strategies, Collier-MacMillan

CRC/ATCDE (1974), Teacher Education in a Multicultural Society, (Reprinted 1978 by the Commission for Racial Equality)

D.E.S. (1971), The Education of Immigrants, (Education Survey 13), H.M.S.O.

D.E.S. (1977), Education in Schools - a consultative document, H.M.S.O.

Derrick, J. (1977), Language Needs of Minority Children, N.F.E.R.

Driver, G. (1977), "Cultural competence, social power, and school achievement: West Indian pupils in the Midlands," New Community, Vol. 5, No. 4

Driver, G. (1979), "Classroom stress and school achievement," in V. Saifullah Khan (Ed.), Minority Families in Britain, Methuen

Edwards, V. (1978), "Language attitudes and underperformance in West Indian children," Educational Review, Vol. 30. No. 1

Edwards, V. (1979), The West Indian Language Issue in British Schools, R.K.P.

Gibbes, N. (1980), West Indian Teachers Speak Out, C.T.A. and Lewisham C.R.C.

Giles, R. (1976), "Black power and black studies," C.R.C. Journal, Vol. 4, No. 6

Giles, R. (1977), The West Indian Experience in British Schools, Heinemann

Hastie, T. (1981), "Encouraging tunnel vision," The Times Educational Supplement, (6 March)

Harmingson, D. (1973), Towards Judgment, (C.A.R.E. Occasional Pub. No. 1.)

'James Report' (1972), Teacher Education and Training, H.M.S.O.

James, A. (1979), "The multicultural curriculum," N.A.M.E. Journal, Vol. 8, No. 1

Jeffcoate, R. (1979 (a)) Positive Image, Writers and Readers Pub. Co-op.

Jeffcoate, R. (1979 (b)), "A multicultural curriculum - beyond the orthodoxy," Trends in Education, 4

Klein, G. (1981), "Multicultural imagination," The Times Educational Supplement, (9 January)

Lister, D. (1980), "Black teachers face bias in jobs and promotion," The Times Educational Supplement, (3 October)

Lister, A. (1981), "Increasing awareness of racism," The Times Educational Supplement, (6 March)

Little, A. & Willey, R. (1981), Multi-Ethnic Education: The Way Forward, Schools Council

McNeal, J. & Rogers, M. (1971), The Multi-Racial School, Penguin

New Society, (1978), "Race and Teachers," (16 February)

N.U.T. (1967), The Education of Immigrants, London

N.U.T. (1979), In Black and White, London

Parkinson, J. & McDonald, B. (1972), "Teaching race neutrally", Race, Vol. 13, No. 3

Pidgeon, D. (1970), Expectation and Pupil Performance, N.F.E.R.

Rosenthal, R. & Jacobson, L. (1968), Pygmalion in the Classroom, Holt, Rinehart & Winston

Rist, R. (1970), "Student social class and teacher education," Harvard Educational Review, Vol. 40, No. 3

Rose, E.J.B. et al (1969), Colour and Citizenship, O.U.P.

Select Committee on Race Relations and Immigration (1973), Education, H.M.S.O.

Stenhouse, L. (1975), "Problems of research in teaching about race relations," in Bagley, C. & Verma, G. (Eds.), Race and Education across Cultures, Heinemann

Stone, M. (1981), The Education of the Black Child in Britain, Fontana

Tomlinson, S.(1981), Educational Subnormality, R.K.P.

Townsend, H.E.R. (1971), Immigrant Pupils in England: The LEA Response, N.F.E.R.

Townsend, H.E.R. & Brittan, E. (1972), Organisation in Multiracial Schools, N.F.E.R.

Townsend, H.E.R. & Brittan, E. (1973), <u>Multiracial Education: Need and Innovation</u>, Schools Council

Vennig, P. (1981), "New right movements," <u>The Times Educational Supplement</u>, (13 March)

DISCUSSION

This was a wide-ranging discussion, and again the focal points have been extracted and are indicated below. In general, comments and observations tended to concern multicultural education in schools, rather than the research implications for teacher education.

1. ## Aims and objectives

     Several participants made the point that many teachers and teacher trainers, as well as pupils and their parents, have an assimilationist view of multicultural education, and do not necessarily fully understand or share a commitment to cultural pluralism. Nor is there a full realisation that an increasingly interdependent world requires a global view of resources, policies and human relations. An explicit recognition of cultural diversity is reflected in the recent DES paper, *The School Curriculum* (1981), and there is a major research and development task ahead in devising strategies in teacher education, and in the schools.

2. ## Teaching ethnic minority pupils

     The recent report by Stone (1981), referred to in Dr Tomlinson's paper, gave rise to considerable discussion, and in particular the suggestion that schools should concentrate on offering ethnic minority children traditional, basic 'teaching', leaving such matters as culture maintenance and cultural identity to the minority communities themselves. This seems to imply that teacher attitude is of less importance than some evidence suggests, and the view was expressed that teacher education perhaps needs to produce teachers who are both informed and caring and also well trained and competent in subject teaching. This might be an important area for future research.

3. ## Teacher attitudes

     Britain's imperial past has undoubtedly left a legacy of assumptions and perceptions which are now out of tune with the contemporary social and political context. Teacher education clearly needs to sensitise students in initial and in-service training to the hazards of ethnocentrism, and to include in its curriculum the study of intercultural prejudice and racism. Research might well contribute to policy in this area. Indeed, the point was made that Dr Tomlinson's view that "... there would seem to be no need for further research on teacher attitude and opinions," is arguable; and that more probing studies of teachers' perceptual frames of reference and particularly in their dealings with white pupils, are urgently needed.*

4. <u>Future research and social policy</u>

The discussion drew attention to relevant research in other disciplines: for example, psychological studies of cognitive style, and work in linguistics. There was also felt to be a need for further research in areas such as the following:

- patterns of learning <u>within</u> as well as between ethnic and social class groups

- the perceptions of ethnic minority pupils and their parents, assessed by means of participant observation studies within minority communities

- the effect of multicultural education on the attitudes and work of both minority and majority culture schoolchildren

Points were also made about the resource implications of developing relevant research and development policies, especially in teacher education; and about the need to demonstrate public recognition of work in multicultural education by upgrading posts in this field.

---

* A point more fully developed in a comment subsequently submitted by Dr P M Figueroa (mimeo., University of Southampton)

Chapter Four

PRESENT PROVISION IN INITIAL TRAINING

Derek Cherrington & Ray Giles

This paper describes the authors' national survey of multicultural aspects of teacher training, carried out in 1979. It is complemented, in Chapter Nine, by the report of a 1980 sample survey.

In 1979, we conducted a survey in all the Colleges of Higher Education, Polytechnics and Universities offering teacher education in the U.K., to obtain information about courses dealing with multicultural education.[1] The survey produced statistical data showing the location, types, level and duration of courses, and also some general information on any current or longterm plans for course development, research, publications, staff development, projects or resource centre developments. An additional outcome of the survey is a directory of contact persons who can supply details of courses and other activities in these institutions.

The data in the report should be considered against a background of contraction in higher education and especially in teacher education. This contraction is evidenced by a reduction in recruitment levels, financial cuts which affect staffing levels, staff development programmes, and course development as a whole. Secondly, the majority of higher education institutions are not self-validating, and initiating new courses, in multicultural education for example, can take some time. Similarly, during a period of financial restraint Local Authorities exert some influence over the priorities of the institutions they control, and this can have a deadening effect on course initiatives in such fields of study as multicultural education. However, within that depressing background, there are groups of academics who see themselves as having a role in developing a multicultural curriculum. The authors hope that the survey will enable them and others working in this field of teacher education to extend their network of contacts, and to exchange and develop ideas with a view to new and further course developments.

---

[1] Giles & Cherrington (1981), funded by the Commission for Racial Equality

Obviously, surveys of this kind do of necessity have
to operate within a rigid time frame and as a
consequence are invariably dated when published.
Their long term value lies in creating a reference
point from which subsequent progress or otherwise can
be charted. Also, by publishing a directory of survey
contacts, a potential network is created for use by
people active in a field of study, and this can be an
invaluable mechanism for the exchange of ideas and
information.

Since no other national survey in this field in
initial teacher education had been conducted, it was
decided that the survey would collect basic data and
lay the groundwork for a system of continuous updating
of such data should the CRE wish to do it. The project
began with an initial letter and a 'contact person
sheet' which was sent to the heads of all the
institutions. The letter and contact sheet were sent
out by the CRE as it was felt that such a letter would
have more authority coming from the office of the
Deputy Chairman, and would greatly enhance the level
of returns. Returns from the initial contact letter
enabled the researchers to (a), construct the
directory of contact persons, and (b), to establish a
direct contact for the second phase of the survey. A
survey instrument was designed and was sent to each
contact person, asking him/her to provide details of
any multicultural education programmes or activities
being offered in that institution. Follow up
procedures were used with all institutions who failed
to respond either to the initial contact letter or to
the survey instrument. Finally, an analysis of
responses to the survey instrument was carried out.

The National Provision of Courses

The following are the findings with reference to each
of the three broad groups of higher education
institutions:

(a) Colleges and Institutes of Higher Education

14 different Colleges reported having a total of
26 different courses for multicultural education.
Of these 26 courses only 4 were listed as
compulsory. On the other hand, there were 46
different courses which were described as
containing elements related to multicultural

education. These were the combined offerings of 17 different colleges. Of these the majority were compulsory. It would appear that the majority of students and teachers following programmes offered through colleges which emphasise multicultural education, would receive it through compulsory offerings in the foundations and methods courses.

In these institutions, there does appear to be a growth of activity in the generation of courses which include some element of multicultural education. It would also appear that the main thrust for development is coming from those colleges which are either situated in or serve large urban conurbations. In terms of new developments and plans, it would appear that some colleges are at the stage of re-negotiating the content of courses, especially those validated by the CNAA. The level of new activity does reinforce the view of the researchers that the directory of courses generated by this project should be periodically updated otherwise it will rapidly become outdated.

(b) Polytechnics

There were 18 different courses offered by 9 different Polytechnics, and again, only four were described as compulsory. There were a number of offerings in the area of multicultural education which were not designated as courses or elements. There were, however, comments to the effect that 14 such units of instruction were compulsory. In these institutions, too, there does appear to be a steady growth of new courses and other developments in the field of multicultural education. It should perhaps be noted that many Colleges of Education merged with Polytechnics in the mid-1970s, and that by now they will be re-negotiating the validation of their CNAA courses for a further five years. It is likely that we have identified many of the new proposals, but is is equally likely that many more will be in the pipeline in the next twelve months.

(c) Universities

There were only 4 courses on multicultural

education offered by 4 different Universities. Only one (offered at Brunel) was designated as compulsory, ('Multicultural Education'). There were also 13 courses identified as having elements related to multicultural education at 9 different institutions. Only 3 were designated as compulsory, most were not designated compulsory or optional.

With some notable exceptions, there appear to be few obvious new initiatives being taken in this sector of higher education. It may well be that economic restraints operated on this sector of higher education first. A number of institutions indicated that as they were not involved in teacher training they would perforce have to send in a nil return, but this did not necessarily mean lack of interest in the area, as evidenced by research activities. There would also be a number of general undergraduate courses available, dealing with race and urban problems, but these were often not listed as they did not fit within a teacher education rubric.

Course Design and Content

There were two basic approaches for the inclusion of multicultural education into the curricula of various programmes for teacher training. Either multicultural education was offered as a separate course of study, as a part of the programme for the B.Ed. or the Diploma in Higher Education or the Post Graduate Certificate in Education; or multicultural education elements were included in some of the compulsory or optional courses in the various programmes.

As far as content is concerned, there were two different strategies in evidence for both courses and elements of courses. First, there were courses and elements of courses which helped to prepare teachers to understand and teach about Britain as a multicultural society. A number of institutions offered specific courses for this purpose, for example,

- 'Education for Life in a Multicultural Society' (Bath College)

- 'Historical Background to Multicultural Britain' (Bradford College)

- 'Education for a Multicultural Society' (Christ's College, King Alfred's College, Edge Hill College, Leeds Polytechnic, Manchester College, Preston Polytechnic, Leeds University, Roehampton Institute)

- 'Education in a Multiracial Society' (Derby Lonsdale College, Luton College, Worcester College)

- 'Multicultural Education' (Dorset Institute, Roehampton Institute, Keele University, Brunel University)

- 'English in a Multiracial Society' (Manchester College)

- 'Education in the Multi-ethnic Society' (North London Polytechnic)

- 'Education for a Multicultural Britain' (Keele University)

On the other hand, many courses and elements of courses were presented to help teachers and students develop special competencies for teaching in schools or classrooms with racially or culturally diverse pupil populations. For example,

- 'Teaching in Multicultural Schools' (Bedford College)

- 'The Multiracial School' (Ilkley College)

- 'English in the Multiracial School' (Manchester College)

- 'Teaching in the Multicultural Classroom' (North London Polytechnic)

- 'Community and Race Relations' (Bradford College)

There were also courses and elements of courses designed to address the needs of specific populations. For example,

- 'Language Problems of Various Ethnic Groups' (Worcester College)

- 'Education of Minority Groups' (Edge Hill College)

- 'Education of the Disadvantaged Child' (Manchester College)

- 'Education of Children of Ethnic and Racial Minority Groups' (Wolverhmampton Polytechnic)

- 'Education of Special Cultural Groups' (Bristol University)

Identified Groups or Topics

Looking at the titles of the various courses and the descriptions of the elements of courses categorised as 'multicultural', we found a number of specific social groups identified and a variety of themes or issues covered under a number of different disciplines. For example:

(a) Groups

The following groups were referred to specifically as the topic for courses or elements of courses offered by institutions responding to the survey:

Africans, American Negroes, Asians, the disadvantaged, immigrant peoples, minority groups, religious groups, Welsh.

(b) Topics

Among the various issues cited as topics for consideration in courses as a part of multicultural education were the following:

English as a second language, comparative education, race and education, equality of educational opportunity, urban education, Caribbean literature, attitude formation and the nature of prejudice, minority group children in British society, barriers to learning, identity, treatment of minority groups, migration, race relations, religious and moral education, world religions, African studies, Asian studies, the child in the human situation, language across the curriculum, community education, Third World studies, children with special needs, school and community, compensatory and remedial education.

Conclusions

One of the major findings of this survey of multicultural courses in teacher training institutions was that the terms multicultural and multi-ethnic education were used in very limited ways. Without exception, these terms were employed to develop approaches for equalising educational opportunities for children presumed to be disadvantaged because of cultural and/or linguistic differences; or for teaching about the culture of ethnic minority groups, either to members of those groups in order to improve self-image, or to other groups and the wider population in order to create cultural awareness and to improve race relations.

Both these approaches focused on the presence of highly visible minority groups in British society, who are seen as having difficulties in school and in the wider society. The sudden urgency of the need to find a solution to these difficulties has resulted in the terms multi-ethnic and multicultural education taking on a considerable amount of emotional and political appeal. Many teacher training institutions have thus justified the need for the establishment of supportive programmes to help teachers work more effectively with the disadvantaged and to improve race relations.

Because of the way information was collected for the survey, it is not possible to determine whether any of the colleges which train teachers look at the organisation of the school and at the institutional racism inherent in many of the policies and practices of the school system, as a part of the problem. Although schools in many areas serve predominantly black and cultu ally disparate pupil populations, the curriculum in any of these schools continues to reflect an a mption of cultural and ethnic homogeneity. Tea rs are frequently confounded by the verbal and oth behaviour patterns of ethnic minorities which do not conform to the 'accepted' behaviour patterns associated with the potential for academic success. These, coupled with language difficulties and the racism inherent in much of British society, lead teachers to have lower expectations of black pupils (especially those of Afro-Caribbean descent) than of white children of the same socio-economic background. Moreover, many studies have shown that teacher expectation is closely linked to pupil performance. In the relatively few teacher training institutions which have responded to the challenge of multicultural classrooms by offering specialist courses, most titles suggest that the 'problem' lies with the school children, rather than in the severely limited capacity or willingness of either the schools or most teachers to respond to a new situation. Many institutions present multicultural education as an approach for dealing with a 'problem', rather than an educational concept valid for all children in a multicultural society.

Almost all of the courses and elements of courses described as multicultural or multi-ethnic which are offered by the teacher training institutions, are concerned with cultural content focused almost exclusively on the background and heritage of black groups to the exclusion of all others. This approach, however well intentioned, results in black groups being perceived in isolation from the dominant white society. Thus, in addition to being a highly visible minority group, the emphasis placed on their cultural differences serves to reinforce their being viewed as a separate part of the British society. Consequently, multicultural courses also tend to be seen by many student teachers and tutors as an examination of the problems faced by black people in white British society. Obviously, the most desirable way to approach education for a culturally plural society would be to widen the cultural content of the teacher training syllabuses to reflect elements representative of all the various cultural groups which comprise the United Kingdom. The findings of this survey do not indicate that any steps are being taken in this direction.

While the concept of multicultural education has the potential for various types of application, the current practice seems to be directed towards the stated goal of equalising educational opportunity for black pupils, and educating the white British population about the cultural characteristics of that group and other ethnic minorities recently settled in Britain. One obvious assumption underlying both these approaches is that cultural differences are the bases of educational disadvantage and racial prejudice. This approach gives minor attention to the greater role that ethnocentrism and racial discrimination play in creating the disadvantages minorities face, and it also fails to provide an adequate analysis of the structures which create the disadvantages for these pupils.

For multicultural education to become regarded as a valid educational concept for all schools in multicultural Britain, it must be expanded from a purely problem-oriented, subject-based approach. The entire school curriculum is culturally biased. What needs to be pointed out is that the history of Britain is one of interaction with many other peoples, and that British culture in all its forms has borrowed from and been influenced by other cultures from the earliest recorded history. This should be emphasised in the subject matter of every course taught in British schools. Only by helping teachers to become aware of, and to convey this perspective to all pupils, will the present bias which reinforces prejudice and racial discrimination be eliminated. Further surveys of teacher training institutions should be focused on what is being done to help teachers change the way all subjects in schools are being taught; and to indicate how such institutions are themselves addressing the problems of discrimination on their campuses, rather than to merely determine how many teacher training institutions have grafted on multicultural courses as options or inserted elements in other course offerings.

Suggestions for Further Research

The presentation or offering of courses in multicultural education, by itself, should not necessarily be interpreted as a commitment of the various institutions surveyed in this study to the concept of multicultural education. In addition to the curricula of the teacher education programmes which were surveyed in this enquiry, attention needs to be given to several other areas which also affect the way in which multicultural teacher education may be effectively carried out. For example:

(a) Institutional policy

How do the institutions' philosophy statements address multicultural education? What policies reflect a commitment to multicultural education? How does an institution determine whether its staff have a commitment to the task of preparing teachers to live and work in a multicultural society? Is there a person or a committee designated to develop a plan to systematically design, implement, evaluate, monitor and report on the progress of the integration of multicultural education within the teacher education programme? Does the budget reflect support for multicultural education?

(b) Staffing and staff development

How is the current competence of teaching staff in the field of multicultural education determined? What efforts are being made to increase the competence of staff in this area? What outreach programmes have been developed to assist local schools with change efforts related to multicultural education? What aspects of multicultural education are addressed through such programmes? What incentives encourage staff to plan, develop and integrate multicultural education into their areas of responsibility?

(c) Resources and facilities for teacher education programmes

What resources in the library allow for an examination of topics, themes and concepts related to multicultural education? What are the acquisition policies for purchasing and displaying multicultural resource materials? What criteria are used for evaluating materials for their racial, ethnic and sex biases? How does the library quantitatively and qualitively support the instruction, research and service needs for multicultural education?

(d) Evaluation, course review and planning within teacher education programmes

What multicultural components are included in the systematic evaluation of graduates? How are the results used to improve multicultural education components of the teacher education programme? In what ways does the long range plan reflect a commitment to multicultural education?

These and other questions should be the subject for a more detailed investigation of multicultural teacher education programmes.

Chapter Five

PRESENT PROVISION IN IN-SERVICE TRAINING

John Eggleston

This Chapter offers a preliminary account of the most recent large-scale enquiry to have been undertaken into the in-service education of teachers for work in a multicultural society.

At Keele University we have recently undertaken a major DES-funded enquiry on In-Service Teacher Education in a Multi-Racial Society, and this Chapter presents a very small part of our findings for consideration. The origins of our work and the motivations for it are to be found in the context of the House of Commons Working Party for the Eradication of Colour Prejudice. Indeed, a concern for the elimination of prejudice was a dominant feature throughout the conception and undertaking of the activity, as the preamble to our original paper made clear.

"Deeply embedded in the culture of British society are prejudices based upon racial differences, particularly those of colour. For the most part these operate at a more diffuse and subtle level than can be reached by even the most effective legislation. Yet they bring about a level of discrimination that has major effects on the lives of many thousands of citizens. There are unmistakable economic as well as humanitarian justifications for the eradication of such a state of affairs in work, in leisure, in community and in the wider society by all possible means and for its substitution by a wider and more embracing tolerance."

It was to the work of the teachers that the proposal addressed itself especially. It stated that in the past decade,

"... schools and their teachers have shown an increasing awareness of their important responsibilities in this area, endeavouring in their work to challenge prejudice and to substitute it with a tolerance based upon more

objective understanding of fellow human beings.
The work of some schools has been outstanding,
predominantly, but by no means exclusively, in
multiracial districts where problems connected
with race have been conspicuous and often urgent.

At the heart of the matter is the work of the
individual teacher. His skills, his sensitivity,
his professional performance and his level of
concern may powerfully diminish racial prejudice.
Equally it may leave it untouched or even,
inadvertently, exacerbate it. An initial
exploration of the roots of colour prejudice
cannot ignore the role of the teacher: indeed it
could hardly begin at a more opportune place. The
proposal that follows examines the ways in which
teachers may be more fully equipped for work in a
multiracial society."

In the light of this advocacy the proposal had little
difficulty in identifying the area for research - in-
service teacher education.

"In recent years, an increasing number of in-
service courses has been made available for
teachers facing the issues and problems of
teaching in a multiracial society. A wide range of
provision has arisen, including short and long
courses with full-time or part-time attendance,
that lead to an equally wide range of achievement
and qualification. Familiarity with a number of
these courses as visiting lecturer, external
examiner or assessor, has brought the writer to a
keen appreciation of their quality and the
enhancement to professional knowledge and
sensitivity to which they may give rise. Yet
though much good is clearly being achieved by such
courses, we have very little detailed knowledge of
their efficiency and relative effectiveness. We
also lack a clear picture of their origins and
specific objectives, their recruitment and
distribution, their content and methodology and,
above all, their consequences in the communities,
schools and classrooms. At a time when there is a
widespread acceptance of the need for further
development of in-service courses in multiracial
education, there is a disturbing lack of firm
evidence on which policies may be based."

In the two years since the commencement of the project the arguments used in the initial proposal have come to have even greater force. The multiracial characteristics of Britain have become increasingly evident in work in schools, in community, entertainment and every aspect of everyday life. The proportion of the population comprising ethnic minority groups has increased in size and also in mobility. Yet their problems have also been exacerbated by the difficulties in employment and also in community affairs. Schools have occupied a crucial position. In parallel with these changes the significance of in-service teacher education has also been enhanced as the flow of new entrants to the teaching profession has diminished and, in a number of schools, ceased. Response to change becomes more and more inescapably the responsibility of the existing teaching force.

For these reasons the research has been conducted with a firm conviction of its importance and necessity. It has also been helped by the parallel development of a wide range of other enquiries into the opportunities of ethnic minority groups, including some reviewed by Clarke (1980). Further enquiries have been directed towards particular issues such as Norma Gibbes' (1980) study, West Indian Teachers Speak Out. A study of the availability of courses for teachers in multicultural education has been undertaken by Giles and Cherrington, for the Commission for Racial Equality, and reported in Chapter 4 of this volume. All these and many other studies have not only enhanced the work by the relevance and timeliness of their findings, but also have enabled the research team to identify itself as part of a wider community exploring these crucial issues.

Research Strategy and Implementation

Let us now turn to the overall strategy which guided the project throughout its execution with only the most minor modifications. It is perhaps simplest to present it in its original form as embodied within the original proposal.

"A detailed study of in-service courses on aspects of multiracial education will be drawn. The courses would be examined under the following broad headings:

1. Recruitment

   Here issues would include examination of the
   strategies determining the selection of
   teachers, and the circumstances in which
   teachers themselves become willing to
   participate in such courses. Any special
   professional characteristics of the teachers
   recruited would be noted, as would the
   characteristics and distribution of schools
   from whence they came. The availability and
   use of secondment for various courses would be
   analysed, and an attempt would be made to
   explore decisions being made between entry to
   the different courses available.

2. Content of Courses

   Here study would be directed to explore the
   specific purpose of the courses, the ways in
   which they are planned to achieve these
   purposes and the ensuing experiences of course
   members. Analysis would be made of the
   background and experience of those teaching
   the courses. The evaluation of courses by
   tutors, validating bodies and by the
   participants themselves would be considered.

3. The Consequences of the Courses

   Here work would be directed to the
   consideration of the professional role of
   course members in the immediate period
   following the course. How are they deployed by
   LEAs?   Do they return to their original
   schools or elsewhere? Is their work redefined
   to make specific use of their experiences? Do
   they and others see themselves as being
   enhanced by specific skills or sensitivity in
   the field of multiracial education?   An
   attempt will be made to evaluate the degree of
   enhanced effectiveness of teachers, including
   those who have undertaken previous courses.

Overall, the data would be analysed in order to
assemble as compete a picture as possible of the
origins, nature, distribution and efficacy of in-
service courses for teachers, and the results
would be presented in a manner that would be of

value to teachers, LEAs, HMI and all others
concerned with the practice and administration of
education in a multicultural society."

After a lengthy series of negotiations within the
House of Commons Working Party for the Eradication of
Colour Prejudice, with organisations concerned with
minority group interests, with professional bodies,
and with many schools and colleges a final version was
drawn up and approved by the Department of Education
and Science. A grant was offered to the University of
Keele to undertake the work which commenced in
December 1978. A steering committee to guide the
project was drawn up in consultation with officers of
the Department of Education and Science, including not
only members of the Department but also
representatives of LEAs, colleges, polytechnics,
teachers and other organisations, and a member of HMI
who acted as assessor.

Overall, we believe that the project has achieved what
it set out to do. The objectives were set out in the
following passage in the original proposal. "The end
product of the project should consist of a far more
complex knowledge of in-service teacher training for a
multiracial society. It should be able to answer in
detail such questions as "Who participates?", "What
happens to them?" amd "What are the consequences?".
It should offer illumination on the relative merits of
different course modes. It should enable valuable
features of some courses to be made available more
widely. It should offer evidence of any
maldistribution or shortcoming in provision, and
indicate where change or further development is likely
to be most fruitful. It should give some indication of
the overall supply and demand situation for such
provision. In short, it should offer valuable raw
material for the necessary policy decisions in our
educational arrangements for the multiracial society
in Britain in the 1980s."

Demand and Response

Our investigations have left us in no doubt about the
fragmentary and incomplete provision of in-service
teacher education for a multicultural society.
Indeed, it is non-existent in many areas and in none
is it wholly adequate. The evidence is equally clear
about the substantial potential demand for in-service

courses for preparing teachers to work in a
multicultural society. The need for such courses is
most evident in the experiences of many of the
teachers we have interviewed, faced with the day-to-
day and minute-by-minute problems of working in
classrooms with children whose cultural, community,
intellectual and linguistic situations are diverse and
which they only incompletely understand. Often these
situations are shared by all children, resulting in a
classroom that has far more difficulties for the
teacher than those which would arise simply from the
presence of ethnic minority children alone. Quite
apart from their day-to-day problems, many teachers
have keenly felt professional needs to identify and
develop new styles of teaching that are more
appropriate for a multicultural society; these include
considerable numbers of teachers who are not
themselves teaching many pupils from ethnic minority
groups.

Other researchers share these views. The findings of
the Schools Council project, <u>Multi-Ethnic Education:</u>
<u>The Way Forward</u> (Little & Willey 1981), indicate that
many of those responsible for and involved in multi-
ethnic education within LEAs and in schools, now
believe that the presence of minority ethnic group
children has implications which go beyond the need for
special arrangements and special provision, and involve
the curriculum generally. Curriculum development in
these schools is now seen less in terms of simply
adding on special teaching such as 'black studies',
and more as involving a reappraisal of the curriculum
as a whole to make it relevant to all pupils. "Within
Authorities in multiracial areas, there is now wide
agreement that the presence of minority ethnic groups
in Britain has implications for the curriculum in all
schools whatever their ethnic composition,"
(<u>Op.cit.</u>).

It is not only teachers who need the extension of in-
service course provision in this field. Some LEAs,
particularly (but not exclusively) those in areas with
relatively large ethnic minority populations,
urgently seek improved and enhanced expertise in the
teaching and the administration of their schools. The
minority communities and the organisations
representing them are deeply concerned about the
achievements and performance of thir children in
schools; they may also be concerned about the wider
attempts being made in the schools to develop amongst

<u>all</u> a consciousness of diversity within British
society. But perhaps the heart of the demand springs
from the minority group children themselves and their
urgent needs to achieve more satisfying and fulfilling
experiences within the schools where they spend so
much of their early formative years.

Yet such a compelling set of needs does not, alas,
mean that all courses are full and that long waiting
lists are stimulating extended provision. On the
contrary, course providers regularly advised us of
'sluggish' demand, unfilled or even cancelled courses;
some LEA advisers justify low provision on the grounds
of low demand. There are a number of reasons for this
all of which appear to call for action. Firstly, the
communication network in the schools is still
spasmodic. Awareness of any course depends upon the
almost random chance of information reaching the
school, reaching the noticeboard and being read by
staff concerned. Communications through advisers are
sometimes highly effective, but there is little
evidence of any systematic attempts to ensure that
such information is fully available to all possible
participants. A particular problem is that messages
seem to reach teachers who already have some awareness
of their needs more easily than those who do not; the
cynical, the apathetic or the prejudiced. The
situation is exacerbated by the irregularity of
provision. Few providing institutions offer regular
courses; this is particularly the case for short
courses. Moreover, the changing nature of courses
makes any kind of continuity of demand difficult to
establish. Particular problems occur when the
providing institution is outside the contact network
of the LEA in which teachers work. In consequence
recruitment is often local, when the needs of teachers
may be better served by travelling a modest but
feasible distance beyond their LEA boundaries. (There
are also a few occasions where the converse is true.)
A national information network, possibly along the
lines of the weekly page on 'School to Work' in the
<u>Times Educational Supplement</u> may well be the optimum
solution, bringing together not only news of courses
but also of developments in the area, augmenting and
diversifying much of the sort of information that
organisations like N.A.M.E. make available for their
members. Such a feature would of course constitute an
area of in-service provision in itself. Financial
implications would probably not arise; the existence

of such a network would go a long way to ensure the willingness of course providers, authorities and teachers to write for it and read it.

Secondly, the demand from teachers is not always effectively translated into entry to courses. There are many impediments, springing from personal and financial commitments. Release patterns vary between LEAs, and where attendance involves full-time release, replacement staffing, or the payment of fees outside the bounds of LEAs, it is clear that many teachers are impeded if not totally prevented from attending courses. But there are many more subtle but equally effective impediments. Lack of support by a head for a particular course or even any course is likely to deter all but the most enthusiastic teachers, (though there are one or two cases where the hostility of the head seems to have acted as a positive spur to teacher attendance!). The role of the LEA adviser concerned (multicultural education adviser, subject adviser or others) is often equally crucial. Advisers can play a particularly important part on behalf of the LEA, in generating and mobilising a demand from teachers, offering them encouragement, incentive and support in their application and subsequent participation. The availability of colleagues who have experienced similar provision and their evaluation of a course may have a crucial effect in determining a teacher's attendance. Usually such impediments or incentives are spasmodic, personal and highly subjective. We conclude that all LEAs should identify a clear policy of courses which they wish to support and have the resources to support, and establish clear criteria both for selection and encouragement of teachers to participate in them. Advisers and heads should be active supporters and proponents of such a policy of which they will themselves have been participants in establishing.

Thirdly, teachers themselves are, properly, selective. We have already noticed that, understandably, they respond to convenience and financial support. But they are also sharply aware of a range of other professional needs. One is clearly the relevance of the course to their teaching situation, whether in the classroom or in the head's office. Teachers may wish to develop a wide range of specialist fields, whether in curriculum subject, pastoral care, community relationships or administration. Some teachers are of course themselves tutors or potential tutors for in-service courses. There may well be occasions when in addition to teachers and tutors, other members of the education service may enrol. These could include administrators, advisers and teacher centre wardens. Or there may be appropriate special courses for such personnel and in particular for head teachers.

Not all courses, however, are planned in close consultation with teachers, either in their subject and professional organisations or even individually. In a number of cases, the capacities of the course providers or even their entrepreneurial skills seem to be the central determinant of what is offered. We recommend that all courses without exception should be planned with full and visible consultation with groups of teachers who are either past or prospective students or who are well able to represent potential course participants. Moreover we conclude that except for the very short, one-off courses, that these arrangements should be properly institutionalised by LEAs and other providing bodies.

A further concern to many participant teachers is the degree of recognition they are likely to achieve by course attendance. By this we mean not only formal recognition in terms of degrees or other awards or certificates of attendance and the currency they enjoy, but also the informal but no less important recognitions that surround their subsequent professional situation. It is vital that proper recognition of participants as teachers who have special professional expertise and understanding in multicultural education should be accorded to them; that heads and other colleagues should recognise their enhanced expertise to be of use within the school, and that this knowledge should be given the high evaluation and status that it properly deserves. In this connnection, we have noticed that there seems to be a tendency for the more visibly selective entry courses to offer higher status implications than the "open door" ones.

It is now widely recognised that effective teaching in multicultural situations is not a job that 'anyone can do'. But it is equally important to recognise that a short course is not 'all that is needed'; such a belief devalues not only the teachers but also the courses. We conclude that employing Authorities in their appointment and promotion procedures should make full and proper recognition of in-service achievements in multicultural education, and that the qualifications and experience of teachers be featured in any published account of schools in speech days, reports and the like.

There is an urgent need to increase the recruitment of minority ethnic group teachers not only generally into the teaching profession, but also to participate in in-service courses for multicultural situations. Such teachers may have valuable expertise concerning their own groups and situations, but may be unable to relate this expertise to wider issues. They can therefore benefit from courses, while their presence enhances the courses themselves. We conclude that an active policy of recruiting minority group teachers to in-service courses in multicultural education be followed.

We have found that despite the encouragement from HMI and the teachers' organisations the recruitment of teachers from schools and LEAs with relatively few children from minority groups is largely non-existent. This accords closely with the findings of the Schools Council (1981) report, Multi-Ethnic Education: The Way Forward:

> "... although the DES now argues strongly that all schools, whatever their ethnic compositions, should reflect in their teaching the presence of minority ethnic groups in British society, there is little evidence from the findings that any systematic consideration has been given to this in LEAs where there are few or no minority ethnic group pupils."

Yet our study confirms that such teachers have hardly less urgent needs to be aware of the implications of the multicultural society in their own teaching. We conclude that the provision of short courses for teaching in largely mono-ethnic schools be given an urgent national priority by DES. Particular attention to the content, titles and publicity for such courses needs to be given to facilitate recruitment.

Content and Organisation

In most courses under review there was an implicit or explicit view that the main task of schooling

considered was to give recognition to cultural
diversity. Little attention was given to skills,
except basic linguistic skills for pupils learning
English as a second language. There is an equally
urgent need for in-service training that focusses on
helping minority group children to experience and
achieve in more advanced work, including work for
public examinations, and we strongly recommend to
providing bodies that far greater attention be paid to
ensuring that appropriate courses be mounted.

We occasionally encountered the view that courses
should devote more attention to white pupils. The
complexities of aims and content already inherent in
the provision have meant that the specific situations
of white pupils have received little attention.
Nevertheless, it is important that their existence and
any special needs, particularly in schools with a high
proportion of ethnic minority pupils are considered by
providers.

Perhaps most centrally, courses must help teachers to
perceive more fully life as it is seen by the children
and parents of minority ethnic groups, and to
juxtapose this perception against the perceptions of
those of the white majority groups. With these
perceptions must be blended those of the teacher.

Undeniably the crucial ingredient of all courses is
that which enhances the sensitivity of teachers to
children. Though general to all courses of in-service
teacher education and indeed to the whole process of
teaching, it is of transcendental importance to in-
service teacher education. Though it is an elusive
course content, difficult to identify in most
programmes, it is unquestionably true that without it
little else can be achieved.

For all this to happen effectively the participants
must be more than a self-help group. The course
providers must themselves have relevant and up-to-date
experience not only of the situation in a
multicultural classroom, but also of life in
multicultural communities. Almost everywhere this
will require augmentation by inviting teachers with
special expertise (recent members of the course,
ethnic minority teachers, parents and others from the
minority communities and so on) to augment the
knowledge input to such courses. Such inputs, always

important, are also relevant where provision is being made in areas of low minority group concentration.

In the area of knowledge content our conclusions are therefore unambiguous: to ensure that the information presented is sensitive to the needs of the teachers, their classrooms and above all their pupils it must be illuminated not only by up-to-date theoretical understandings (to which we shall refer subsequently) but also by up-to-date experience. This may, and indeed should, be capable of being offered by the staff of providing bodies. Yet there are many situations where they will need to be augmented by practising teachers, particularly those from minority groups, and by other adults in membership or with intimate knowledge of the components of the multicultural community. We conclude that all course providing institutions take special care to ensure their inputs fulfil these requirements, and that teachers and LEAs satisfy themselves that they are so ensured.

Such provision must be school-oriented, directed to the needs and practices of participants and their institutions. It is important that this is not directed in a prescriptive way, but rather in a manner that encourages participants themselves to innovate and build upon the experiences of their schools and of the course. Course content must always be related to the community served by the school, again not in a prescriptive way but in a way that allows communities to link with the school to the advantage of the education and the opportunities of all their children. Not always do courses of in-service training have the breadth of vision and purpose appropriate to this task.

It is hazardous to make recommendations on the financing of in-service courses in the difficult and fluid conditions of national and local financing. We hope it is also a statement of the obvious to mention that a very high financial priority should be accorded to in-service teacher education for multicultural situations. A particular problem, however, arises from the preference of many LEAs to contain financial commitments within their boundaries. This may take the form of using resources in local polytechnics or colleges (especially if these appear to be underemployed overall), or by providing wholly internal short courses served by present LEA staff. Such arrangements may well offer financial advantage, but they may deny teachers the range of choice or expertise they need. We conclude that LEAs develop at least an informal network of "pooling" finances for courses in multicultural education, so that a national or at least regional pattern of provision can be set up, instead of the distorted and incomplete set of arrangements to which predominantly locally-contained financing can give rise.

Range of Administration of Provision

We have shown in our report that the range of provision and its distribution largely arises by the chance incidence of local and even personal initiatives, rather than through co-ordinated policy. Our evidence of the need for courses and the potential demand for them leads inexorably to the conclusion that the DES takes steps to ensure that, ultimately all teachers, but immediately those teachers in the major conurbations, have the opportunity to participate in short courses and, with minimal delay, in longer courses also. An increased opportunity for participation in relevant part-time diploma courses, is also a major objective. There is also a clear case for a far greater range of opportunities to undertake part-time B.Ed. courses in the field of multicultural education. Even in some of our major urban areas there is a severely limited range of in-service provision for multicultural teaching at anything beyond the short course level.

In exploring the range and administration of courses we have once again reiterated our conclusions for an overall national, regional and local provision. The objective is nothing less than to make an understanding and appreciation of the issue of multicultural education available to all teachers. Yet it is important not to see such conclusions as a case for grandiose schemes of nationally all-embracing provision. The realities of the present day situations - professional, administrative and economic - would make this a nonsense even if we were to advocate it. But we do argue that a far fuller and ultimately comprehensive availability of courses be built upon present foundations, that arrangements for far more effective co-ordination be instituted formally or informally between DES, LEAs, other providing bodies, teachers' organisation, schools, the minority communities and all other interested parties. We also reiterate our earlier argument that in the light of such developments, a far more effective information service be available to teachers so that they are not denied the opportunity to benefit from the provision through incomplete or inadequate information as happens, alas, all too often in the present situation.

Consequences

The consequences of the courses we have examined are, inevitably, some of the most elusive results of our study. The consequences of all educational activities are notoriously difficult to ascertain. They are well known to be predominantly long-term rather than short-term, and of course all the courses we considered are still in a relatively early stage of existence. Moreover, education is never a unique or even an independent variable. Certainly our evidence shows that the extent to which a teacher's subsequent professional performance is enhanced by the course is greatly determined by the policies of LEAs and their advisers, by the attitude and degree of support of heads and heads of departments, and by the general ambiance, social condition and ethos of the school.

Yet notwithstanding these constraints there was significant evidence of change in the thinking and perception of very many of the participants. Many were able to convince us of an enhanced sensitivity, an experience of professional stimulation and increments of confidence for working in multicultural situations. Many participants were able to provide evidence of their increased self-awareness, for example, in the examination of their own assumptions, in their capacity to identify racial bias in textbooks and, perhaps most importantly, in their enhanced capacity to establish a rapport with ethnic minority group children in their schools and classes.

There was also evidence of change in the motivation of many participants. Though perhaps this is not surprising as, to some extent, those who attend courses of these kinds are a self-selected group, likely to be more willing to respond to the professional purposes of the course, we nevertheless detected a noticeable shift from what might be called "assimilatory" goals to those that could be described as "culturally pluralist" goals. Moreover we detected shifts from rather generalised enthusiasms to understand and appreciate the issues, to positions of enthusiasm for positive, professional teaching skills of use in multicultural situations. There was particular enthusiasm for the acquisition of skills in curriculum development.

In these areas of enhanced professional skills, however, the evidence of successful acquisition did not often match the evidence of enthusiasm to acquire them. We found little indication that, on leaving the course, teachers became characterised by particularly effective abilities in any of them. Their capacity to help minority group children in language skills, other than at a fairly elementary level, was not in evidence; neither was their capacity to devise relevant and sensitive curriculum programmes leading to enhanced skills and attainment. Few teachers seemed to be able to display a developed capacity to identify and diagnose in any clear and objective way the special problems of their children other than at a fairly general and often elementary level. Teachers still displayed a tendency to 'leave it to the experts', particularly in the areas of language, assessment and attainment.

Our evidence also indicates that there was little systematic attention paid to the relationship between teachers' understandings and the quality and quantity of students' work. In particular, the emphasis of courses tends to be strongly knowledge oriented (particularly in the field of cultural diversity and its recognition), rather than in the professional skills related to children's classroom performance. Another area of disappointment was that courses seemed to have achieved only limited success in actually enabling teachers to relate better to minority group parents and their expectations of schooling. Here again enthusiasm was not matched by performance. A particular characteristic of teachers who had attended the short courses seemed to be a willingness to settle for somewhat better 'survival skills' rather than to be more determined and better equipped to tackle the major issues of prejudice, differential opportunity and the like.

On almost all courses there is an attempt, explicit or implicit, by tutors to explore issues of personal belief, prejudice and the ideology of cultural diversity. But in far fewer cases is this exploration followed through to a successful conclusion. The task is one of considerable magnitude and in consequence this not infrequently leads to an incomplete and unsatisfactory conclusion or even more commonly, an abandonment of the activity which may be lost in a 'celebration of cultural diversity'. We conclude that far more careful consideration of these issues and the strategies appropriate to them be undertaken by course providers. In particular the complex professional skills needed by course providers to operate in this field need careful development and utilisation.

The need for development of in-service education emphasises issues far wider than multicultural issues, of course. A recent HMI report outlines the wide ranging need for enhanced in-service teacher training and sees it as "no longer a luxury but a necessity", (DES 1981).

Such considerations are underlined by the findings of our report. We have shown that in-service teacher education for a multicultural society is spasmodic in provision and response; that it is incompletely available and in some cases quite unavailable to teachers who seek it. Its knowledge content is uneven, its organisation often irregular, its follow-up unsure. It offers virtually nothing for teachers working in predominantly mono-ethnic situations. Conversely, minority group interests are often virtually unrepresented. It must be emphasised that our study can only examine what is visible above the tip of the iceberg; as a deficit analysis it is thus incomplete.

We have developed a compelling case for an extended provision of in-service education for a multicultural society. But we have also argued the case for a far more coherent and comprehensive organisation of provision on national and regional lines. This is essential in order to ensure continuity, comprehensive revision, and financial arrangements that do not distort demand and supply; appropriate recognition and accreditation of teachers; proper participation in course planning and effective follow-up. Only in this way can we establish the effective core of our society's provision for a genuine multicultural education: sensitive, well informed and properly

qualified teachers committed to the development of a
sound multicultural society, a society in which
diversity is welcomed for its positive benefits rather
than being rejected, trivialised or romanticised.

REFERENCES

Clarke, L. (1980), The Transition from School to Work:
a critical review of research in the United Kingdom,
London: HMSO

Clarke, L. (1980), The Practice of Vocational
Guidance: a critical review of research in the United
Kingdom, London: HMSO

Clarke, L. (1980), Occupational Choice: a critical
review of research in the United Kingdom, London:
HMSO

Department of Education & Science (1981), Teacher-
training and the Secondary School, London: HMSO

Gibbes, N. (1980), West Indian Teachers Speak Out
Their Experiences in Some of London's Schools, London:
CTA and Lewisham CRC

Little, A. and Willey, R. (1981), Multi-ethnic
Education: The Way Forward, London: Schools Council

DISCUSSION

The paper by Derek Cherrington and Ray Giles, and that by John Eggleston were followed by a single discussion session in which the main issues (indicated below) ranged across both means and ends in initial and in-service teacher training.

1. Definition of the field

    As in earlier sessions, the definition of the field was a significant element in the discussion. Once again it was stated that multicultural education in initial and in-service training involves more than the study of black immigrant groups, and the development of competencies for meeting the special needs of immigrant children. Nor is it necessarily centrally concerned with equipping teachers to provide 'black studies' curricula for black pupils born and raised in Britain, and to meet special educational needs of a more subtle kind. (There is, in any case, a much broader spectrum of ethnic minority groups in Britain, including the Irish, Italians, Polish, Cypriots and Jews). Multicultural education involves the larger question of conveying to teachers an informed sensitivity towards cultural diversity, and of developing competencies for operationalising this in the classroom for all children in all regions of the country.

2. In-service courses

    An extensive and coherent programme of in-service education is an essential professional support if teachers are to work effectively, whatever the ethnic composition of their classrooms. The potential demand for multicultural courses is very considerable; but the courses are not always adequately publicised or equally accessible to all teachers, and they are not always framed so as to meet the real classroom needs.

3. School-based in-service training

    In some aspects of curriculum development school-based INSET has provided a new dimension and impetus. But in multicultural education, in-service courses are still necessary in order to provide the groundwork and to generate a number of change-agents in the schools. These courses need to be related to classroom needs so as to attract teachers; having been involved in a consideration of the issues, participants are then in a position to act as catalyst/resource in school-based development. Follow-up work - in the absence of support from the head or LEA - is essential to maintaining momentum among course members. But generating school-based change is always a difficult process; and, of course, multicultural education will be one of a number of priorities in curriculum development for many teachers.

4. Needs in teacher education

It was felt by many seminar participants that teacher educators at both initial and in-service levels are in need of:

- a substantial updating in the appreciation of the contemporary significance of multicultural education in the professional education of teachers

- an informal professional network for the exchange of ideas and experience about in-service strategies, course content etc.

- a more sophisticated grasp of relevant theoretical concepts and bodies of knowledge on which to base professional practice. Too often the existence and the content of a course on multicultural education is related to the availability and interest of individual tutors. The Keele survey identified some good practice, but overall the courses were rather patchy.

- and, perhaps most important, a systematic programme of in-service training, a 'training the trainers' exercise.

Chapter Six

VIEWS FROM TEACHER EDUCATION

The following two papers are by tutors engaged, respectively, in initial and in-service teacher education, and each represents a personal commentary on needs, opportunities and constraints in this field.

A Multicultural Perspective on Initial Training

Alan James

In my work in initial teacher education, I have always eschewed separate 'multicultural' courses or bits of courses, be they optional or compulsory, rather to the surprise of like-minded colleagues in other Colleges, and of committed teachers, HMIs and others; but I think I can persuade them that, in the long run, the slow and patient process of transforming the entire programme is the only way to achieve the aims that I would set for teacher education in the multicultural context. My antipathy towards such special courses originated when I first came into teacher education, and inherited a course which was offered to second year students on Tuesday afternoons as one of a range of activities as heterogeneous as guitar playing and rock climbing. The 'hidden curriculum' located it as either a soft option; or at best, as a source of tips for dealing with some rather peculiar children that you might be unlucky enough to meet on teaching practice, and/or as an ornamental addition to the College reference for employers. More fundamentally, it became clear to me that no matter how exciting, sensitive or challenging I might seek to make the course, there was no virtue in trying to make it a compulsory element in the teacher education programme. It would have stuck out in grotesque isolation, far removed from the perceptions of most of my colleagues at that time, and a source of suspicion and resentment for a substantial number of students.

As the old Certificate of Education was painfully transformed into the B.Ed. degree, the Tuesday afternoon circus died, and I set to work on the slow, frustrating process of permeating the College B.Ed.

programme with multicultural awareness. It seems to
me that there is now much more chance that students
taking our B.Ed. courses will become aware of the
nature of the multicultural society they are working
in, of the delicate ways in which children's attitudes
towards themselves and others are shaped, and that
they will have been prompted to think about the
implications of this knowledge for their work as
teachers. Even more important, I feel that
'multicultural education' is ceasing to be seen as a
specialism, an arcane body of wisdom invested in a few
experts; it is recognised as an essential aspect of
the students' ethical and emotional orientation
towards the job of educating. This is not due only to
my own efforts; I have more colleagues now who have
taught in multicultural schools, and others who have
extensive knowledge of and commitment to such fields
as comparative religion, world development studies,
Commonwealth literature. These and others have
succeeded in integrating into their own philosophies
of education, into their own conceptions of childhood
and of society, their awareness of cultural diversity,
their ability to 'taste the drunkenness of things
being various'.

A Policy Statement

In 1978, the following statement of policy for teacher
education in a multicultural society was adopted by
the College's Education Division, and I have set it
out in full for I shall be referring to its various
elements later on in this paper.

I   <u>The professional responsibilities of a teacher
    in a multiracial society</u>

    A.   It is a teacher's responsibility to know
    and understand the children he teaches to
    the best of his ability.

        In particular, to know and understand those
    social and cultural elements of an
    individual child's upbringing and
    experience which contribute to the
    formation of his distinctive personality,
    and to accept and to value these
    distinctive characteristics, so that his
    understanding of them informs the content
    and methods of his teaching of *each* child.

B.   It is also a teacher's responsibility to develop his understanding, throughout his career, of the complex and changing nature of society, and of the knowledge, attitudes and skills needed by children growing up in such a society, so that his understanding of these informs the content and methods of his teaching of all children.

('A' implies a special responsibility for any teacher who is teaching a child of ethnic minority background (such children are by no means peculiar to the obviously 'multiracial' schools in inner urban areas); 'B' implies a responsibility for *all* teachers of *all* children to prepare those children for life in a multiracial society. Thus, these statements entail a common set of objectives for the initial vocational education of *all* teachers.)

II <u>A Statement of objectives entailed by para.I above</u>

A. <u>Affective</u>

On completion of their initial vocational education, all student teachers should *accept* and understand the practical implications for teachers of:

1. the uniqueness of each human being

2. the elements of common experience shared by all human beings

3. the principles of equal rights and of justice

4. the value of the best achievements of all nations, cultures and civilisations

5. diversity and strangeness as sources of interest and stimulus rather than fear and threat

6. the cultural diversity and complexity of British society in the past, the present and the future

7. the dynamic and constantly-evolving character of all living cultures

B. Cognitive/propositional

On completion of their initial teacher education, all student teachers should know, and understand the practical implications for teachers of:

1. the meaning in scientific usage of the terms 'race', 'culture' and 'community'

2(a) the historic reasons for the cultural diversity of modern Britain, and in particular, the reasons for immigration of various ethnic groups during the 20th century

2(b) the identity and main distinctive characteristics of major cultural minorities in present-day Britain, including their religious and social customs, the character and status of their languages, and their moral and cultural values

2(c) the ethnic composition of the area served by the College

2(d) the ethnic composition of their home areas

3. the influences which contribute to the development of attitudes towards self and others in a growing child; and in particular, the special factors influencing the sense of identity of an ethnic minority child, and the factors likely to implant or reinforce hostile attitudes towards groups different from his own in any child, and to cause racial discrimination in practice.

C. Cognitive/procedural

On completion of their initial teacher-education, all student teachers *should be able to:*

1(a) recognise, and constantly reassess his/her own attitudes, beliefs and understanding

1(b) participate in rational discourse, argue for or against a case, change his/her mind in response to evidence, argument or experience

1(c) communicate effectively with adults and children whose range of cultural and social experience differs from his/her own

1(d) understand and apply the principles of equal rights and justice in his/her dealings with adults and children

1(e) evaluate objectively the achievements of any individual, cultural group, nation or civilisation, irrespective of whether she/he identifies with it or not.

2.   select sources of learning experience for children which:

   - will be intelligible to each child in terms of his/her own experience and upbringing

   - will enable each child to draw on the resources of his/her own experience and upbringing in a positive way

   - will provide all children with accurate information about the world as it is at present, and in particular the character of modern British society

   - will encourage all children to value the diversity of humanity, and in particular, the cultural richness of a multicultural society, as sources of stimulus and interest

3. detect, in any materials available for children to see, hear or read:

  - factual inaccuracy, especially in the presentation of information about racial and cultural differences

  - stereotyping, especially in the presentation of information about distinctive cultural groups (in Britain and overseas)

  - bias, especially in the interpretation of the values, beliefs and cultural achievements of other nations and civilisations

4. plan and organise his/her teaching so that each child:

  - is helped to overcome specific learning difficulties, in particular, difficulties in the use of English

  - has opportunities to communicate with the teacher and with other children, drawing on his/her own experience and expressing his own ideas, attitudes and beliefs, in the expectation that these will be received with positive interest and valued in their own terms

  - has opportunities to hear and read about the experiences, attitudes and beliefs of others different from him/herself

This policy statement is built in the austere Gothic manner of Bloom's taxonomy, which may be helpful in defining with colleagues precisely what students should be able to do at the end of a course. It is now somewhat dated. I have reservations about some of the items, and am less sure about the feasibility of 'multicultural education by objectives'. However, looking at the statement may help define the current objectives for initial teacher education.

Professional Responsibilities and Cognitive/ Propositional Objectives

The document begins with a statement of 'the professional responsibilities of a teacher in a multiracial society'; this emphasises that the student teacher is an autonomous individual capable of independent decision-making and free commitment to ethical standards. However, the phrase 'to accept and to value' can be criticised as implying that all aspects of a culture which are different from a teacher's own must be 'valued' in an uncritical manner. So readily do students and teachers slip into the habit of listing cultural differences as 'problems' and, at least implicitly, 'defects', that such positive compensation might seem to be desirable. But it has been rightly criticised by Paul Zec, for a sentimental and ultimately nihilistic 'strong relativism' which is essentially as anti-educational as ethnocentrism. Perhaps a more appropriate phrase is Downey's 'respect for persons'; in practical terms for teachers this means looking for distinctive features of a child's own experience in the expectation that these will be more likely to be supportive than destructive, more likely to have a rational basis than an irrational one, and so potentially are more likely than not to be starting-points for educative processes.

A detailed statement of affective and cognitive objectives follows in Part II. Section B sets out some 'cognitive/propositional' objectives which are easier to grasp and to implement in a shopping-list of lectures, essay titles and examination questions, and therefore often tend to become the focus of attention and, sometimes, the end in itself. The first item of 'required knowledge' in Section B implies that there is some positive, precise meaning that can be ascribed to such slippery words as 'race', 'culture' and 'community', hallowed by 'scientific' usage. However, it is not 'knowing the meaning' that is required for a teacher, but the ability to see through the usage of such words, together with an awareness of the ancient deposits of social assumptions that have formed the most complex strata of accumulated meaning.

The second item in Section B presents immigration as an economic phenomenon, emphasising the 'pull' factors rather than the 'push', mainly to compensate for the

folk-beliefs about immigration likely to be held by
most students; and it then describes the major
cultural minorities and their lifestyles in a
'positivist' kind of way. Nevertheless, I am well
aware that to present one version, or a limited range
of versions of 'the' reasons, etc., is indoctrination,
and it is a 'banking' mode of pedagogy. Items 2(c) and
2(d) entail some active 'finding out' by students.
Compulsion is almost certainly counter-productive in
this kind of work, which requires considerable
commitment and sensitivity. Getting students to
examine their home communities, and to understand the
communities served by schools where they are based for
substantial periods, may achieve more in terms of
'openness to culture' than requiring them to study
multiracial neighbourhoods as such. Similarly,
sensitive studies of language-varieties, (their own
and their friends' accents, dialects and so forth),
can be as valuable as studies of bilingualism to
indicate an 'openness to language in all its forms'
(Bullock, 8). 'Multicultural awareness' is only a part
of such openness to human diversity, and it can only
be achieved in the context of a process of teacher
education which fosters such openness across a much
wider range of experience.

The third item in Section B is another pillar of the
present-day orthodoxy of multiculturalism; the
development of children's attitudes towards
themselves and others. I am very conscious that the
models of self-concept and attitude development which
underpinned much multicultural activity in the 1970s
were pretty crude, based on a kind of 'associationist'
psychology which treated children's selves and
attitudes to others as direct products of the
information fed into them - hence the concern with
curriculum content, with images and stereotypes. My
own teaching of multicultural education owes more to
Freud; this is a version that is more difficult to
teach because it takes us away from the solid matter
of curriculum content, towards the ways in which
children are treated, at home and in school; towards
the modes of communication which we use, the ground
rules of the discourse in which we require them to
participate in the process of being educated, and so
exposes to criticism the assumptions of both tutors
and students, and the rules of the games that they
play in the process of teacher education.

Cognitive/Procedural Objectives

Section C deals with the procedural skills which, I feel, come much nearer to the heart of the problem. The first series still seems to express concisely my own ideas of the purposes of higher education in general, and of teacher education in particular. They reflect my concept of prejudice as a form of communicative incompetence and authoritarian dependency, from which we must try to liberate students in an atmosphere as free as possible of domination. They are obviously idealistic, virtually impossible to attain in practice, but they are yardsticks by which all our teaching practices and institutional structures should be judged. I would suggest that many developents in the organisation, teaching and assessment of teacher education courses in recent years have made these objectives increasingly hard to attain, forcing tutors into an ever more bureaucratic role, and I am not convinced that any number of 'compulsory modules' of multicultural content are going to get us any nearer to achieving these objectives.

The second series (item 2) seems to sum up the practical skills that I would consider most important to an aspiring teacher, but these lead on to the more specific demands under item C3, which I now find rather negative in tone. They seem to reflect in this the censoriousness of all those sets of 'guidelines' that have become so familiar in the last few years. There are certainly no excuses for publishers to go on publishing and teachers to go on using out-of-date, inaccurate, offensive books and materials when much better things are on the market. However, there is a risk that activists in the multicultural field may be developing the art of 'hunting the stereotype' to such a degree of finesse that they can find implicit racism in the telephone directory. The tone of some of these guidelines is reminiscent of the Soviet Writers' Union in the darkest days of Stalin, with their prescriptions for what should count as a 'good' book, or even a 'good' author, and what sorts of books (and authors) should be liquidated. This is no way to encourage a healthy response to literature and sources of information.

What is really needed is that students should learn to identify children's books which present the world in ways that celebrate, vividly, truthfully and imaginatively, the richness and complexity of humanity. They ought to spend much more time reading children's literature, fiction and non-fiction, (and less time reading badly-written textbooks of sociology, psychology and the like); learning to recognise that 'truth' in writing is a matter of complexity and contradictoriness, quite out of conformity to any 'guidelines', and that a stereotype is simply a badly portrayed human character, a symptom of sloppy authorship. Then, I think, the fourth series of objectives under Section C might have some hope of realisation. These, again, do entail some fairly specific training in particular modes of class organisation, the use of specific teaching resources, the planning of curricula, lessons and materials. These are undoubtedly specific skills needed by teachers who are going to enable children to break free of the constraints of prejudice and re-supposition, and these skills need to be taught.

Affective Objectives

However, the lists of informational content and procedural skills that have formed the main focus of attention in most recommendations for the education of teachers in a multicultural society cannot be separated from a concept of 'professional attitudes', an ethical orientation towards the job of teaching which entails the kinds of affective objectives listed in Section A. There are several layers of misperception which, I think, need to be peeled away before we can hope to achieve these. The first, that the diversity of cultures in present-day Britain is of no significance for teachers, is quite easily dismissed as irresponsible and blinkered; and the belief that the distinctive aspects of the life-experience of ethnic minority children is of no positive significance, even for the teachers who teach such children, is even more blatantly unprofessional. Although such assumptions still prevail among many members of the teaching profession, even in multiracial schools, student teachers increasingly recognise that they do need to make some kind of response to this diversity.

What kind of response are we seeking? The simplest, perhaps, is to feel sorry for ethnic minorities. Many students seem to have that kind of innocent good naturedness that students of Piaget or Kohlberg would associate with junior school children. Unfortunately,

it tends to lead in practice to the kind of
patronising concern for the happiness of such children
that (as Maureen Stone has argued) distracts attention
from the job of giving those children the skills which
they will need in coping with a less kindly world. A
development of this emotional response is the
fatalistic rationalisation which sees racism and
injustice as matters beyond the sphere of teachers'
influence, suggesting again that we may protect and
cocoon children from these nastinesses, but we cannot
hope to change them. At a slightly more sophisticated
level, the response becomes hostile: the differences
among ethnic groups are 'problems', and the persistent
maintenance of these differences by adults and by the
children themselves makes them the active creators of
their own disadvantages. Sometimes students come to
accept, as if by religious conversion, the particular
version of multicultural reality which we seek to
impose upon them; many multicultural syllabuses entail
a kind of political indoctrination which, if
successful, sends forth students bursting with zeal to
crusade against racial injustice in our schools. This
response may be the most dangerous of all as it denies
the very concept of education on which our aims are
based, by creating another kind of authoritarian
dependency.

The 'acceptance' that is asked for in the series of
objectives under Section A on my list does not entail
acceptance of a specific set of propositions about the
multicultural society as it is today, nor a particular
construction of political reality. What they do
entail is something in a teacher's attitude towards
people in general and children in particular which
goes far beyond mere 'tolerance', to a positive
enjoyment of diversity, complexity and ambiguity. The
'irritable striving after fact and truth' is the
essence of the common humanity shared by all of us,
and the abdication that underlies prejudice and racism
is a withdrawal from that striving, falling back on
complacent assumptions that our truth and our
rightness are simple, fixed and accessible. Educating
teachers, or children, for life in a multicultural
society is far more demanding than any syllabus of
aims, objectives and content can ever suggest, and it
stretches to the utmost our capacity to do the job of
'educating'. It calls for sensitivity, flexibility
and sympathy, not for the arrogant and prescriptive
tones adopted by some of the campaigners for the
multicultural curriculum.

REFERENCES

STONE, M. (1981), The Education of the Black Child in Britain, Fontana

A Multicultural Course for Experienced Teachers

Tuku Mukherjee

I took over the course leading to the advanced Diploma in Education for a Multicultural Society at Southlands College in September 1976. However, my involvement with the course goes back to 1974, when I was invited to become a visiting lecturer, and subsequently the invitation was extended to join the Diploma Tutorial Board. As a member of the Board, I became aware of the broad educational objectives of the course, i.e. to provide a year of intense academic scholarship with visits and lectures, "to develop a theoretical and practical understanding of the implications of education in a multicultural society, and of community relations with special reference to minority groups and the education of immigrant children". The following is a personal commentary on the changing rationale of the Diploma course, and in particular on the centrality of race awareness within it.

The Assimilative Model

My own view then and now is that this Diploma course was a truly 'pioneering' initiative, and the ethos and the content of the course had a definite appeal for me. It seemed to suggest an alternative perspective to education, where the responsibility of a teacher would be to project and reflect the realities of a multicultural as opposed to an ethnocentric Britain. It shifted the emphasis from discord to harmony, from isolation to association. It blended neatly with my then uncritical and sincere acceptance of integration as defined by Roy Jenkins, on 23rd May, 1966, at (where else) the Commonwealth Institute:

> "... not as a flattening process of assimilation but as equal opportunity, accompanied by cultural diversity, in an atmosphere of mutual tolerance".

For a person, who had been involved in community relations for nearly a decade, operating under the subtleties of British racism, mediating as a marginal third man between power and 'black' community and pupils, the definition was the best available, and I held on to it, through most of the first year of the course. The year was difficult, and often quite exhausting. My responses were based on my experience in Southall in west London, as a teacher, as a youth leader, and through my involvement with organisations and individuals within the community. I 'taught as I learned and learned as I taught', and realised how difficult it must be for even the most dedicated teacher to keep up with the current research in the dynamic, fluid field of race relations and multicultural education. It was not until the end of that first year in the summer of 1977, that I was in any position to critically explore not only my own views, but also the whole discourse on multicultural education and my personal role and responsibility as a teacher. I realised that I had changed my locale from Southall to Wimbledon, but my perspective had not changed. During that first year, I had continued to view multicultural studies as a process of integration within the framework of an 'assimilative' model, and I came to realise that I must move from such a position of 'integration' and marginality to one of 'affirmation' within a pluralistic framework. My responsibility, as I saw it then and still do, is to recognise that every person who is seconded to the course is the author of her/his own experience, both as an individual and a teacher. It was and is my duty to provide the security, the confidence, the scholarship, and experiences not only to allow that authorship to articulate with a specific focus on racism and race relations; but also to make the students critically aware of the educational, social and political issues of a multicultural society, and to encourage them to develop perceptive multiple 'antennae' to analyse, examine, interpret and project in their content, and in their method of teaching the realities of a multicultural society. We all have to recognise that education is real and authentic only when it evokes an adequate, creative and critical response to the reality represented by it.

Ethnocentrism and Feeling

I had begun to feel that my 'black' presence on the course with my 'black' experience in Britain which spread over a decade, inevitably injected a new orientation to the course, because skin colour has its own meaning and message. I had brought with me the objective reality of British racism. I would claim that the 'black perspective' is essential to any multicultural course, not only because of our experiental contribution but also because we need to articulate with equal confidence our differing experiences to the children we teach, without becoming 'invisible' just because we happen to be a minority in the staff room. Simultaneously, we need to delearn the process of judging ourselves through white criteria, norms and values.

My own experience of life, as an Indian, suggests that multiculturalism is a state and an attitude of mind. It is not a discipline, and yet it permeates every discipline. It transcends reason, and yet my experience at Southlands indicated quite clearly that the concept of multiculturalism in the 'white' world had been grasped intellectually but not necessarily incorporated in the world of feelings. Intellect is free, capable and willing to accept the concept, but is not free to act. Furthermore, white socialisation and education in an ethnocentric world inevitably leads to a racist and sexist view of life, and clearly indicates a definitive position and how other cultures and peoples are to be viewed and treated. Most are capable of reasoning their way out of the 'binary' position of superior and inferior, but find it difficult to act on their intellectual perception of multicultural education, because the 'cult' of reason in the Western World has more or less destroyed the world of feeling. Multicultural education by its very definition must not only lead to heightened cross-cultural awareness, but activate the subjective world of feelings sufficiently well to enable course members to participate fully in cross-cultural activities. Without this we shall never be able to move beyond an exotic presentation of minority cultures, a superficial package of 'black studies' for 'black pupils', or a multicultural evening produced by 'sleight of hand' at Diwali.

I came to realise that the debate on multicultural education had been out of balance. It had been dominated either by an emphasis on the teaching of English as a second language, or by an obsession with minority cultures, subcultures, religion, customs and traditions. The conscious or unconscious motivating force behind such a presentation was that a study and understanding of minority cultures and institutions would somehow make our presence more 'tolerable' and 'legitimate'. It was a moral appeal made on our behalf. Such a projection follows a predictable pattern of presenting the Asian community as an undifferentiated group of people totally tied to their religion, whose past, present and even future is a blurred continuum; and as people, we emerge as either static or imprisoned irrevocably in our religion and culture. The West Indian community, on the other hand, often find themselves presented as being in a state of permanent muscular tension because of 'alienation' and the 'lack of culture'. Above all, minority children are seen as a 'problem' to be dealt with. Inevitably, the victim becomes the cause, and multicultural education becomes a process and a department to diffuse the tension - the dialectic of information, control and power. Minority, and 'black studies' had often been used by white liberals for the education of the 'black' child, with his community, institutions and people as an object of study and research, either to correct, to expose our deficiency, or to add to the mechanics of control which must feed on knowledge to function. It had become a theory and practice of containment without making any dent in the pervasive assimilative model, or raising the most central issue affecting all our children, both black and white - that of racism.

The Centrality of Race Awareness

With this realisation, for the past few years I have been trying to shift the thrust of the debate and the emphasis. The core of the Diploma course is now firmly rooted in anti-racist awareness and teaching. It seems to me that by a quiet process of consensus, the educational world has remained, until very recently, totally silent on *racism*, and on its devastating and dehumanising effects on our 'psychological world' and on our institutions - probably the most important issue of the twentieth century. I am convinced that racism has its own substance, function and power to humiliate and mutilate right across the colour line. Its effect on the 'black' community is visible, identifiable and quantifiable, but what about the long-term damaging effects on the white psyche? Its pathological effect on whites has been recognised by the United States Commission on Mental Health, since 1965. As they expressed it: "... the racist attitude of Americans which causes and perpetuates tension is patently a most compelling health hazard. Its destructive effects severely cripple the growth and development of millions of our citizens young and old alike". Myrdal's American dilemma of conflict between

what whites believe and what they actually do in their
collusion, conscious or unconscious, with racist
practices, can be transposed and is just as valid for
Britain today as it was for America in 1944. I would
argue that the ethnocentric assimilative model, by
totally ignoring the presence of minority children in
its content, method, curriculum, resources, staffing
and organisation, is racist by 'omission' and that it
is damaging to both white and black. Whichever they
are, they both grow up with distorted notions of their
self-worth, identity and eventual position and status
in society, and the long term effects will be
counterproductive. The sharp focus of ethnocentrism
on the white world which does not offer any
alternative except perpetuation of racist and sexist
ideology and reproduction of class position,will only
accelerate the process of already massive alienation.
One only needs to look at the youth culture to see
this happening.

The educational world needs to be 'modernised', at the
moment, it is 'backward and underdeveloped'. It does
not reflect either the reality of multicultural/
multiracial Britain, or her international dependence
on a multicultural/multiracial power structure.
Britain may have territorially decolonised her empire,
but the psyche, orientation and view of life remains
frozen within a colonial framework. White Britain is
far more in need of multicultural/multiracial
education than is ever admitted or realised except in
White or Green Papers. The 'black' presence is often
seen as a threat or projected as the 'enemy within',
but it offers White Britain the only chance she has to
break free from her 'colonial imprisonment' by
acknowledging that her historical, cultural and
industrial heritage was built on black oppression.
Once that suppressed area of knowledge is allowed to
surface then perhaps we can negotiate a more
meaningful 'inter-dependent model' of education - a
perspective which brings relevance and meaning to our
experience. It is the only model which carries the
logic of national and international survival, and
offers the possibility of resolving the conflict
between unity and diversity, when unity does not mean
uniformity.

Multiculturalism

This vibrating and meaningful multiracial/
multicultural 'interdependent' model of education is

already functioning within territorial boundaries
carved out by minorities in places like Southall,
Brixton, and Brent in London. These areas may appear
to the dominant society as a 'patch of colour', but
each of these collectives represents a diversity of
cultures and peoples with striking differences in
customs, traditions, social institutions and views of
life with its own power structure; and by its very
composition each is multilingual, multireligious and
multicultural, with the oppression of racism acting as
a unifying force. But the model has much wider
implications for British society as a whole. I would
suggest that to redress the present imbalance in
multicultural/multiracial education, we must include
not just minority studies but a critical examination
and evaluation of white society, white attitudes, and
above all, of the crucial issue of white racism, both
individual and institutional, which divides and
incapacitates us from initiating any meaningful change
in our system of education.

I am fully aware that nearly all attending the Diploma
course come with a certain amount of awareness of the
social, political and educational issues raised by the
'black' presence. Once on the course, it becomes our
responsibility - both teachers and students - not only
to inform but also to explore with honesty, integrity,
care and concern, both intellectually and emotionally
the racist/anti-racist attitudes and perceptions we
bring to our awareness, For eventually it will be our
attitudes, backed up with hard information and
evidence, which will determine our responses and
initiatives. To deal with this very sensitive area of
attitude and race, we have developed a 'racism
awareness programme', which draws on Judy Katz and her
research on 'white awareness'. A full analysis of the
programme will appear in due course in New Community.
But very briefly, Ms Katz offers a specific definition
of prejudice, discrimination and racism which we have
been using interchangeably in Britain. She defines
racism as "prejudice plus the power to activate the
prejudice" and locates it as an issue for the white
community. She offers strategies and techniques to
help "... individuals examine their attitudes and
behaviours as whites, and the implications of their
own racism in order to become more fully human". The
black members of the course find it easier to tread
the area of racism because of their experience. But
some whites in the group have found it threatening and

hazardous, for the exercise involves not only an attempt (both as an individual and as a member of a group) to explore the structure of meanings towards black people acquired in an ethnocentric white world, but an attempt also to locate their own participation, either overtly, or by collusion, or by omission, or by abdication of responsibility, in perpetuating racism. The experience may be painful, but if we in Britain are to operate an anti-discriminatory, anti-racist, interdependent multiracial/multicultural model of education then whites must learn to know themselves and what they stand for, just as we blacks had to find ourselves, before they can function constructively and with integrity in such a system.

DISCUSSION

The papers by Tuku Mukherjee and Alan James were followed by a fairly limited discussion involving either macro aspects of the societal role of teacher educators, or micro issues relating to course content. The main points are indicated below.

1. ### Education and society

    Despite the obvious constraints education can influence society, and teacher education consequently has a pivotal role. But in considering educational objectives and the dimensions of social change, the possible definitions of our future 'multicultural society' must take account of the perceptions both of majority and minority culture members. This is bound to be a complex matter.

2. ### Initial and in-service teacher education

    For some participants, Mr Mukherjee's paper introduced a welcome note of realism; for others, it presented an overly simplified view. But the following emerged as significant elements for inclusion in ITT and INSET courses:

    -   an appropriate curriculum for children preparing to take their place in a culturally plural society

    -   a capacity to work with children in the area of intercultural prejudice and racism

    -   a systematic cultivation of respect for ethnic minority cultures

    -   a parallel awareness of the need for social cohesion in a complex society

    -   a familiarity with and competence in utilising appropriate organisational strategies in schools

3. ### Role of the teacher

    During discussion, different aspects of the

teacher's role in respect of his/her work in a
multicultural society, and the implications for
teacher education, were touched upon. Issues
raised included the following:

- the cultivation of positive attitudes
  towards minority groups in all work with
  children, across the curriculum. The
  avoidance of sterotyping and of reinforcing
  stereotypes. Recognition of intercultural
  variations in belief and practice, and not
  merely variations in colour

- the more open classroom. discussion of issues
  relating to discrimination; and the more
  open consideration of techniques and coping
  skills whereby minority group children can
  more successfully fill social roles in the
  world of work

- laying a sound foundation in language and
  literacy skills in particular, to reduce the
  bases of discrimination and to enhance
  coping skills

- the recognition of macro factors outside the
  control of education which inevitably place
  limits upon what is possible in the
  classroom and in teacher education

Chapter Seven

PERCEPTIONS OF NEED BY TEACHERS

This Chapter comprises three papers which have been contributed by practising teachers, and which are based upon their current experience in multicultural work in primary, secondary and further education respectively.

Multicultural Teaching and the Primary School

Jeff White

While some aspects of this paper will be specific to those schools which contain children of diverse ethnic origin, its main considerations are intended to be applicable to all schools.

Any discussion of the multicultural curriculum cannot ignore the fact that all curriculum development occurs within a society of endemic racism. Curriculum reform never really challenges the fundamental perspectives of education, and measures for change are largely considered within the existing educational framework. There is, nevertheless, a sense in which any school which attempts to pursue an ethos committed to pluralism could be said to be challenging the school's traditional role as the transmitter of the dominant culture. This is a very necessary challenge and one which all teachers in their initial and in-service training should be made aware of. While it is recognised that education alone cannot change the power structure of society, we should accept more positively that it can affect the life-chances of children and produce individuals who will question society's dominant norms and values. Some readers of this paper may already be asking, 'what has this to do with primary education?'. The key point here is that even at the primary stage we must determine what education is for, and the question of teacher attitude is of prime importance if we believe that schools should display an informed, sensitive approach to cultural diversity and recognise the equal worth of all cultures.

Pluralism in the Curriculum

There seems little doubt that teachers play a vital role in sustaining prevailing definitions of the value content of the curriculum. Given this situation it is important that for a pluralist perspective to be adopted, teachers should focus upon traditionally held educational concepts and hypotheses and challenge them. The concept of 'compensation', for instance, has had a wide ranging influence on curriculum ideology and terminology in the urban context. It is unlikely that many teachers working in the urban situation have not heard the view that children from low socio-economic backgrounds are cognitively and linguistically 'disadvantaged'. The ideological basis of concepts of this nature which encourage a social pathology view of children and their families must be questioned very seriously. Teachers must be encouraged to ask whether such a view is particularly damaging in the multicultural situation, and whether it tends to justify an ethnocentric approach to the development of knowledge.

Teachers need then to be sensitively informed about the cultures and social structures within their own school community, and to adopt an open acceptance of difference. It should be necessary in in-service training for teachers to regularly re-appraise the curriculum. A concentration upon content necessitates an examination of the whole curriculum, not merely those aspects which can easily be afforded a multicultural dimension. For the primary school teacher, this 'total' concentration should focus upon accepted primary practice such as a thematic approach to learning or aspects of language across the curriculum. The thematic or topic approach can produce exciting and worthwhile work but it has to be utilised carefully. So often, for example, work on cultural 'roots' runs the risk of stereotyping complex historical and socio-cultural patterns. Work of this nature can often re-introduce in the primary school the notion of history and geography as distinct subjects. Themes and topics should demand an integration across the curriculum and produce ongoing resources. The important point here is that the primary school teacher should be asking, 'What view of the world do we want our children to have, and what questions do we want them finally to ask?'

Language Development, and Identity

The whole matter of language across the curriculum in the primary school must be viewed in the wider context of identity enhancement. Unfortunately, there is still the view widely held in primary education that language development should be geared towards 'enrichment' because children in the urban situation are 'linguistically deprived'. As suggested above, concepts of this nature must be seriously challenged. For the purpose of the primary school curriculum, it is not entirely the structure of language that is important but what function it serves and the attitudes of its speakers. Schools reinforce linguistic prejudice if they do not attempt to afford respect and parity for children's home language. For those children who speak a form or dialect of English, the task of the school is to provide situations in which they can initiate language and where the emphasis is upon effective usage rather than upon 'correct' expression. (This includes children of Caribbean parental origin.) Standard English must be seen as only one part of children's communication skills albeit a necessary one. Teachers need, in initial and in-service training, to receive comprehensive instruction in linguistic development so that they develop 'open minds' with regard to children's language. Language development in the multicultural primary school does not simply mean English as a 2nd language.

While children need to be encouraged to be more language conscious so that they can be confident in their chosen mode of expression, teachers also need to be sensitively aware of their own use of language. Unfortunately, the growth in education of language which reifies individuals has played a crucial role in the labelling process which assists the justification of a context that hierarchically differentiates pupils. Teachers need to be encouraged to guard against the use of labels such as 'underachiever', 'disadvantaged', 'slow', 'dull', 'deprived', and so on. These labels, as with the practice of streaming, seek almost to determine inexorably the child's nature. As Michael Apple has said, "Language is both a sensitive indicator and a powerful creator of background assumptions about people's levels of competence and merit." Any labelling which finds fault within the child and encourages the comparison of

performance has potentially dangerous connotations
within the multicultural situation. An acceptance of
diversity does not mean the categorisation of
individuals or groups based upon psychometry.
Teachers' own language awareness could be said, then,
to have an impact upon the enhancement of the child's
own image.

A major role of the multicultural primary school is
the enhancement of self-image and identity. This
should be a central concern of curriculum strategies.
In this respect the visual character of the school is
important, and displays and pictures in all schools
should be representative of the multi-ethnic nature of
society. Much more than this, however, is required if
the curriculum is to enhance a positive self-image in
every child. The whole question of resources has to
be considered. The multicultural primary school
should be aware of the racially stereotyped images
which occur frequently in published resources and
books. While these cannot be eliminated entirely,
teachers should be aware of what questions to ask.
There is little doubt, for instance, that books play a
major role in shaping children's view of themselves
and the world around them. Teachers require in-service
training to develop strategies for entering into
dialogue about the use and suitability of books in
their schools, for all too often both fiction and non-
fiction books are accepted uncritically. Two major
gaps in provision still are the lack of graded readers
reflecting ethnic diversity,and the dearth of primary
school fiction which portrays children of different
ethnic origin growing up together in this society.
Literature in all primary schools could play a far
more significant part in developing children's
awareness of the multicultural nature of society.

Multicultural Teaching

It seems fairly obvious, then, that heightened
consciousness on the part of the primary school
teacher will have beneficial effects upon the
development of the child's positive self-image. This
increased awareness must display itself in all
curriculum areas, so that a multicultural perspective
does not become a special or exotic feature but is the
norm of education. The colourful and exotic aspects of
multiculturalism must be considered carefully. While
not denying, for instance, that Ras and Gurba dancing,
steel band playing, or the celebration of religious

and cultural festivals are important educational
activities, it is to be hoped that they could be
creatively utilised so that there is some movement
forward in the multicultural curriculum. Hopefully,
one day, we will all of us refer merely to 'the
curriculum' and the fact of its being multicultural
will be axiomatic in all schools.

The main focus of this paper, then, is that the
acceptance and encouragement of diversity as the norm
of human progress have to replace existing educational
norms if the concept of multiculturalism is to have
any impact. In other words, we have to develop
teachers who have essentially questioned their own
attitudes and consequently believe in what Dahrendorf
has called the "justice and the creativity of
diversity, difference and conflict." Any discussion
of the primary school's specific curriculum needs is
irrelevant if it does not centre upon the crucial
aspect of teacher attitude. The several points I have
made are summarised below.

(a) <u>essential recognitions</u>

- young children are aware of ethnic
  difference
- schools cannot divorce themselves from the
  question of racism
- teacher attitude is of prime importance

(b) <u>attitudes to be explored in initial and in-
    service training</u>

- the acceptance of cultural diversity as the
  norm of human progress
- the equal valuation of varied backgrounds
- the questioning of traditionally held
  concepts (e.g. 'compensation', 'cultural/
  linguistic deprivation')
- positive expectations of children (i.e.
  resistance to labelling)

(c) <u>curriculum considerations</u>

- content (themes/projects)
- language (acceptance of the centrality of
  diversity)
- the enhancement of identity
- the visual character of the school

- resources across the curriculum
- book provision (i.e. non-stereotypical content)

Multicultural Teaching and the Secondary School

Harry Tomlinson

Discussion about multicultural education has tended to focus on inner city schools in Britain. But according to a Canadian provincial Minister of Education, education for a multicultural society is,

> "... an education in which the individual child of whatever origin finds not mere acceptance or tolerance but respect and understanding. It is an education in which cultural diversity is seen and used as a valuable resource to enrich the lives of all. It is an education in which differences and similarities are used for positive ends. It is an education in which every child has the chance to benefit from the cultural heritage of others as well as his or her own."

Such an education would be better than what we now provide for all our pupils, particularly those who do not have the opportunity to benefit from being educated with pupils from the ethnic minorities.

In this paper, I wish to concentrate on four aspects of my perception of the needs in schools. Firstly, there is a developing uncertainty about how teachers can contribute to the identity and self concept development of black children in particular, because of the nature of their cultural heritage. I shall refer to two recent publications whose arguments teachers and students should consider; both have implications for what multicultural education should be, and present views on the self concept and teacher perceptions. Secondly, I shall look at work in Canada, because the British perspective often seems inadequate even in a European context. This, I hope, will provide an opportunity for consideration of a different perspective. Thirdly, I shall give suggestions for preparation for teaching particular subjects in secondary schools. Finally, I shall examine perceptions from the school level of monitoring attainment and other 'issues', and show how the danger that disappearing resources and other political concerns affecting education may prevent the educational progress that is possible.

Identity and Self Concept

In her recent book, Maureen Stone (1981) suggests that
many teachers who are attempting to build 'good
relations' with ethnic minority pupils and develop
their pride in their heritage and their identity, may
be unwittingly inhibiting their development. Dr Stone
is asking for the more formal methods used in the West
Indies, rather than the teaching methods and
multicultural courses developed by the teachers who
have attempted to meet what they have seen as the
needs of ethnic minority pupils. She also sees English
schools as offering children no real discipline.

Dr Stone implies that multicultural education, as a
concept, has not been analysed appropriately. I would
obviously accept that before multicultural education
can be recognised as valuable, it is necessary to
define what is meant by the phrase, and often this is
not done. Multicultural education is not merely a
means of solving social problems or for preserving the
status quo. It is not teaching English as a second
language, nor community education taking account of
multiple deprivation. More particularly, it is not a
specialism for the less able, nor a means of isolating
ethnic minority pupils from middle class culture which
is the means of social mobility and educational
success in our society. Resistance to multicultural
developments come from those who believe in the
assimilationist perspective, or who believe that all
children should be perceived as equal by 'colour
blind' teachers. There are also those who believe that
implementing a multicultural curriculum is a counter-
productive political act. These arguments must be
countered. Justifications are made in terms of racism
being a pathological disease to be cured and because
the law of the land requires it. The more positive
reasons are that multicultural education is
appropriate for society and the world as it is, and
that it provides a better, more exciting education.
Whatever the educational objectives of multicultural
education they need to be clarified, and not assumed.
There has been a lack of rigorous thinking!

There is considerable interest in the self concept and
the relationship of this to school success. In The
Self in Education, J B Thomas concludes (his words are
only slightly modified) that the research shows that
teachers are a force for good in the field of self
concept, given the will to experiment and succeed. The
self concept can be developed through developing

experimental curriculum projects designed to enhance self worth. More personal and private talk with pupils in a calm, supportive atmosphere and the avoidance of dominating, threatening and sarcastic behaviour is helpful. Teachers who become more person-orientated in the classroom are successful. They can elevate the academic self concept of pupils through combinations of actions, gestures, comments and other cues, through which the pupil perceives the teacher's opinion of his ability to do homework and to realise educational aspirations. Teachers who seek to understand children and to facilitate their growth and development seem to enable pupils to perceive the self-concepts of fellow pupils more objectively, hence schools could begin to reduce racism. Through such teacher-pupil relationships, education can provide experiences which will enable pupils to become objective, open and accepting to all experiences whether unfavourable or favourable to the self. These arguments I accept more than those of Dr Stone.

The Canadian Perspective

Toronto has a multicultural population which has grown in a similar way to that of some British cities with (in 1977) 30% of the pupils born outside the country, and 40% with a language other than English as their first language. The views expressed in The Impact of Multi-Ethnicity on Canadian Education (D'Oyley 1977) are described below.

The final report of the workshop on multicultural programmes of the Toronto Board of Education made clear the teachers' responsibilities relating to racism, as follows:

"Under certain stress conditions such as those presently with us of inflation and unemployment, unconscious discrimination can become active prejudice, which in turn leads to the ugliest forms of racism. For these reasons, educational institutions should support the initiated efforts to have it eliminated.

It is evident that while the elimination of racism is everybody's affair, it is the specific business of education to confront it squarely, and to do everything in its power to prevent it from rooting itself either in the school institution or in the personalities of its students.

Racism or racial prejudice cannot be dealt with in
the subconscious; there must be opportunities to
bring the problem to the area of consciousness in
order to deal with it reasonably ... there is a
pressing need for opportunities for staff to
explore their own feelings, bring them to the
level of consciousness and to deal with them
reasonably."

Social and personal education courses in British
secondary schools should take account of this.

The Ministry of Culture and Recreation has inaugurated
a multicultural history project and is collecting,
processing and making accessible in the Archives of
Ontario, archival material about the history of all
the more than seventy ethnic groups in the Province.
It will publicise their important contributions, and
encourage the publication of multicultural histories
of all ethnic groups in the Province. The resulting
works will be well researched, scholarly and popular,
and should go far in dispelling misconceptions and
prejudices. The potential positive long term impact
of this project is much greater than the haphazard and
uncoordinated developments occurring here in Britain.
Twenty languages are taught for credits in Toronto
secondary schools. The relationship between cultural
and linguistic experiences is recognised and in this
and other ways, positive efforts are made to build on
the links between language and education. There is
considerable surprise that the question of bilingual
education has been restricted in Britain to discussion
of the needs of Scottish and Welsh pupils. This is
still largely so, and the importance of the first
language for a child's emotional and intellectual
development is still not recognised sufficiently in
Britain. All teachers of ethnic minority children in
Britain need to be much more aware of their language
needs which the Bullock Report made quite clear.

Students on the B.Ed. programme at York University
spend one day a week in a school from September to
March, and a two to five week period in that school in
April, May. In the three years course the student has
long-term experience in three different schools,
usually at three different levels, and almost all
students spend at least one year in an inner city
school with a multi-ethnic population. The first year
course "Communication and the Education Process" helps

students confront their own attitudes, biases and stereotypes, usually in discussion groups, using filmclips portraying social situations dealing with attitudes to and stereotypes of age, sex, occupation, class, religion, race and culture. The end product is intended to be increased self-knowledge, and sensitivity to and understanding of other people's differences.

A Canadian, Paul Collins, suggested four areas of skills he regarded as especially critical for teachers in a multicultural society:

- "Ability to analyse his or her own cultural roots; the processes which have shaped his or her life; the biases, whether they be filtered through racial, social class or linguistic screens; and the values which control personal transactions.

- Ability to analyse the nature and quality of his or her interaction in multicultural settings; between self and students, self and colleagues, self and parents.

- Ability to foster interaction among pupils of multicultural settings.

- Ability to teach ethnic content which deals with value-laden issues of injustice, power, racism, discrimination."

Perhaps if all teachers in Britain were trained in these four skills we would make considerable progress, and particularly if more experienced teachers were given the opportunity for in-service training.

Preparation for Subject Teaching

There is no academic institution primarily concerned with education and research about the Caribbean, and the Society for Caribbean Studies at its annual conferences is the only means in Britain for developing appropriate relationships between academics, teachers and active community participants. Such an institution would provide the academic environment in which teachers could gain the academic knowledge required by historians, geographers, linguists, social scientists and social anthropologists if they are to teach effectively about the Caribbean. There is too much teaching in schools of the history and geography in particular of the West Indies, based on secondhand knowledge only.

Home economics teachers need to overcome any lack of background knowledge of the dietary laws and food habits of their pupils. Dress and' fabric work, child care and family relationships, personal hygiene and personal relationships are other aspects of ethnic minority cultures which home economics teachers need to be aware of. With such a perception, teachers of classes with ethnic minority pupils should have increased sensitivity, and teachers of classes of white pupils should be able to broaden the understanding of their pupils through an improved home economics curriculum. A similar argument apples to teachers of subjects such as literature, history, geography, social sciences, religious education, and social and personal education also. A multi-ethnic community in a school provides a better basis for providing an appropriate curriculum for pupils growing up in Britain today. Religious education, like the other humanities subjects seems to be most effectively taught through themes such as the transition rites, birth, puberty, marriage and death, or concepts such as worship or sacrifice. Four arguments have been used for teaching world religions. Firstly, the unique area of religious or spiritual experience is best studied through a range of phenomena with family resemblances from different religions. Secondly, attempts to answer ultimate questions have deeply concerned religions and concern pupils as they develop, and awareness of the perspectives of different religions enables pupils to make better judgements. Thirdly, international understanding includes an understanding of religions, as an important aspect of culture, and is often approached in parallel with a study of global problems such as poverty and conflict. The fourth argument is based on our living in a plural society where such study promotes understanding and mutual tolerance through better community relations, but more acceptably enables pupils to examine fascinating examples of living religions which can be studied at first hand. Such arguments may be developed for most subjects which directly relate to man's personal experience, including the aesthetic areas such as music, art and drama.

Monitoring Performance

Recent research in Manchester suggests there is cause
for concern when black pupils who indicate favourable
attitudes towards their schools continue to be over-
represented in the lower ability bands of those
schools. There seems to be a possibility that the
unfavourable self-stereotyping found in black pupils
by some researchers may be affecting pupils' self-
esteem, motivation and consequent achievement. Race
and intelligence have been said to be related with
unacceptable evidence, but the test results of West
Indian pupils in Redbridge and nationally are a cause
for concern. The National Union of Teachers is not to
cooperate with an Assessment of Performance Unit
survey of the achievements of West Indian children,
partly in the belief that teachers in schools can
identify needs. There is a considerable amount of
research and the conclusions are varied (Tomlinson
1980), but there is little evidence that teachers can
satisfy the needs even if they can identify them. My
belief, however, is that the more evidence there is
the better teachers will be able to attempt to provide
an appropriate education. Monitoring the
effectiveness of school courses has not begun, and
teachers must be prepared for a thorough examination
of the effects of their teaching.

There are now B.Ed. courses in multicultural studies,
but I suspect that there is little such work required
of postgraduate students. In the City of Birmingham
Polytechnic course, for example, there are courses on
the historical backgrounds and present situations of
ethnic minorities in Britain, including society and
social change in Britain since World War II;
multicultural studies including philosophical,
sociological and psychological approaches, and
curriculum studies, with some comparative studies and
theoretical approaches to the study of inter-
culture/race relations; interaction in school and
society, including teachers and children in
multicultural classrooms, and language and minority
groups. Perhaps Dr. Stone would welcome such courses
for teachers already knowledgeable in teachable school
'subjects', but the development of similar courses as
initial training might justify her fears. Perhaps
there is a middle way.

In this paper I have concentrated on the needs in
initial training, but all that I have said has
important consequences for in-service training for the
teachers now in post in all schools.

REFERENCES

D'Oyley, V. (Ed.) (1977), The Impact of Multi-Ethnicity on Canadian Education, Toronto: The Urban Alliance on Race Relations

Stone, M. (1981), The Education of the Black Child in Britain, Fontana

Thomas, J.B. (1980), The Self in Education, N.F.E.R.

Tomlinson, S. (1980), "The educational performance of ethnic minority children", in New Community, 8, 3.

Multicultural Teaching and Further Education

John Gaffikin

For the purposes of this paper, I am taking the phrase 'further education' to mean the non-school, non-advanced education provided by the state and L.E.As for people mainly in the 16 - 19 age group. This education is by full-time, part-time day, block release and evening attendance patterns. It caters for people requiring literacy and numeracy to 'A' level/OND equivalent. The courses can be vocational, non-vocational, or a combination of both. Although my experience does not include higher education nor very much with mature students, many of my comments may also be applicable to that area of post-school education.

The F.E. sector has a long standing interest in the provision of education in a multicultural society. Classes in many areas became ethnically and culturally mixed in the middle 'sixties, and there is probably a stronger tradition of change and adaptation in the F.E. sector than in schools. The C.R.E. booklet, <u>A Second Chance</u>, published in 1976, made the following general observations:

- substantial numbers of students from ethnic minorities use the further education service

- this use is very patchy, i.e. some courses recruit large numbers of minority group students, while on other courses in the same college such students are rare

- such students are more often to be found on full-time courses than on day-release courses, and more often on lower level full-time courses than on advanced ones

- students from minority communities are more likely to embark upon, and remain on, courses beyond the usual age for these courses

- students from ethnic minorities have a higher failure rate in examinations than indigenous students

- ignorance about what F.E. has to offer is
widespread, but ethnic minorities are even more
likely to be unaware of the status and
significance of such qualifications as OND, HND,
NNEB, or COS.

The limited statistical evidence that is available
bears out these impressions.

Teacher Education and F.E.

As a general rule, the teacher training experience of
F.E. staff is either that provided by Colleges of
Education, Colleges of Higher Education and
Universities, or that provided by the specialist F.E.
teacher training colleges of which there are four.
Some of these are now constituents of Colleges of
Higher Education. Those trained via the F.E. college
provision have followed one-year full-time courses, or
two-year part-time day-release or evening courses,
often of an 'in service' nature. To put the situation
in perspective, only 35% of teachers covered by the
F.E. regulations (includes higher education) have
received professional teacher education (NATFHE
1981).

Before I outline the more specific needs that I
perceive, a major general need is that all teacher
education courses must have a multicultural dimension,
and that this component must be as *compulsory* as any
other components that are deemed compulsory. I
recently had a conversation with a trainee teacher who
claimed not to know of the existence of the
multicultural option at her college. My recent
experience as a one-year diploma student in a College
of Higher Education would also indicate that a high
proportion of teacher educators are themselves in need
of re-education in terms of the changed cultural and
ethnic constitution of our society. In-service
training is necessary also for many inspectors,
advisors and L.E.A. officials. The college that I
attended has one of the major and most effective
multicultural education units in the country; and yet
its impact on the mainstream work within the college
appeared much less than it ought to have been, if the
academic board and senior staff had recognised the
value of its work.

My demands of a teacher (stronger than perceptions of

need!) in a multicultural society comprise the following four elements:

- factual knowledge
- an appropriate attitude to the students
- an appropriate attitude to the curriculum
- an appropriate personal life-style

To take each in turn:

(a) Part of any teacher education course should be an up-to-date survey of fact and terminology in relation to the population of this country. Demography, settlement patterns, population movements, cultural and religious practices must be explained and related to childrn's and student's experiences and the consequent impact upon their behaviour, attendance etc. Many supposedly informed visitors to my own institution (Brixton College of F.E.) on viewing upwards of five hundred black students at any one time, are astonished to learn that we have only twenty-two overseas students. They then think our students are some odd category of immigrant. The last thing they think of is that they were born and bred in South London and are as English as the enquirer. It is obviously not possible for all new teachers to be aware of local peculiarities, but it is surely possible for them to be aware of the broad pattern.

(b) Teaching practice must give the trainee teacher the opportunity to develop the appropriate attitude to the student. It is obviously asking a great deal of a course to do this in one year, especially with mature students, but the attempt should be made. My main concern is that many teachers have lower expectations of students from ethnic minorities, and may also be taken aback by a group composed totally of students from an ethnic minority. Multicultural perspectives involve coping effectively with unexpected mono-cultural situations. It is also vital for classroom discipline and personal relationships that teachers are not condescending towards their students. Many teachers consciously (or subconsciously) feel that they are superior or better educated than their students, and are really doing them a favour by being in the classroom. Racial and ethnic differences can compound this barrier. The atmosphere in some teacher education colleges furthers this elitist attitude. Teachers must also be aware that most of our present students received their early education in the period 1970-75, when inner city schools suffered severe staff shortages and a high turnover of staff. The scars still show in terms of attitudes to the system. At the initial teacher training level, my requirements of a teacher would place a great burden on the interviewers and selectors of potential students, for people's life-long attitudes are rarely immediately apparent at eighteen years of age.

In schools and colleges in the U.K., one in seven hundred teachers are black, while one in twenty-five children are from ethnic minorities. NATFHE evidence to the House of Commons Race Relations and Immigration Sub-Committee rightly states that "such a disproportionately low number of teachers is harmful to the establishment of a socially just and fair society, and seriously hinders the development of positive self-images among black children themselves. In addition, it can lead to a reinforcement of the stereotyping which goes on amongst some white children and adults". College interviewers should therefore see membership of an ethnic minority as a positive advantage; and Institutes of Higher Education should attempt to involve themselves with 'access' courses, which involve mature people of an ethnic minority without the usual qualifications for entry, being accepted on to a pre teacher education course run at a college of F.E., and subject to satisfactory progress, being accepted by the institute.

(c) Teachers should have an appropriate, flexible attitude towards the curriculum. In F.E., the replacement of many traditional examinations by those run by the Technical Education Council and the Business Education Council has resulted in much more flexible student and teacher-based programmes of study. Many curricula are now designed by staff committees reporting to an Academic Board and thence to T.E.C. and B.E.C. The latter now recommend and often insist on an integrated approach to the teaching of various subjects, and this places burdens on many staff used to teaching a subject in isolation. Apart from being aware of the opportunity to ensure that the curriculum is multicultural, staff are required, often painfully, to examine their own education and subject and to make adjustments in the light of rapidly changing educational and social circumstances. So it is essential that a flexible attitude to the curriculum is inculcated in teachers at the earliest possible stage, i.e. during their training. Student teachers must be encouraged to feel that they will be initiators of curriculum rather than the agents for passing it on.

(d) The personal life-style of a teacher is obviously a controversial issue. On this, my comments will be highly subjective and some of my opinions strike at the root of professionalism. Many F.E. college educational and disciplinary problems are often the result of class differences: generally middle class teachers are lecturing to working class students. The lack of communication is exacerbated when there are ethnic and cultural differences as well. As a general rule, I think it is desirable that staff live within the catchment area of the college. They then use the same shops, transport facilities and social amenities as the students or their parents, and this does create more of a community spirit within an educational establishment and lessens tensions. The reverse situation is where staff commute from predominantly white suburbs into the cities, bountifully bringing their knowledge and expertise to the aid of the less able, the disadvantaged and the culturally and ethnically different. I do not see that trainee teachers should be encouraged to think that they are going to be 'special' or 'different', because they are going to teach. They should be encouraged to give full rein to their interests and abilities, and use them for the benefit of the community which pays them their wages.

REFERENCES

NATFHE (1981), NATFHE Journal, March issue

DISCUSSION

The discussion following the papers on 'Perceptions of need by teachers' which were given by Jeff White, Harry Tomlinson and John Gaffikin was again fairly limited in scope, and tended to centre upon staff development issues as is indicated below.

1. <u>Staff development in multicultural education</u>

   A variety of ideas were exchanged under this general heading, among them the following:

   - there needs to be compulsory, not optional, provision in all initial teacher education courses

   - there needs to be relevant in-service provision (and the appointment of appropriate advisers) for all-white schools and LEAs, and not only in multi-ethnic areas

   - with the decline in initial training, appropriate in-service provision is now of greater relative importance

   - who should be responsible for the promotion of staff development programmes in this field? The individual school might periodically review its teaching practices, and maintain a rolling programme of staff-release, secondment and school-based work. Or should there be some appropriate regional mechanism to stimulate provision within those LEAs/schools where an awareness is lacking?

   - within the individual school, it is the role of the head or his/her deputy to take responsibility for multicultural education, and to maintain links with the LEA adviser, teachers' centre or regional tertiary institutions. The average class teacher has neither the time nor energy to keep track of local developments and opportunities

   - teachers who have examined and analysed

their own intercultural prejudices, and have developed multicultural curricula/ materials can help and advise others informally and through their participation in INSET

- teacher (and pupil?) exchanges between schools/LEAs in areas of varying concentration can contribute to experience, ideas and insights in this field

2. Training of F.E. teachers

Courses recruit less well among teachers in further education than in the primary and secondary sectors, because many F.E. teachers lack qualified teacher status; and because there may be a greater chance that posts will have changed or even disappeared during a teacher's absence. There also appears to be less LEA interest in funding secondment or release in further education.

3. Biculturalism

This is a topic which was considered at several different points in the seminar. During this session, the arguments in support of mother tongue and culture maintenance programmes designed to promote intergenerational continuity and to preserve a valuable national resource, were balanced by suggestions that biculturalism may also be problematical for individuals, and may even sometimes contribute to social conflict.

Chapter Eight

AN LEA VIEWPOINT

Reg Hartles

LEAs provide educational services, employ teachers and contribute to their initial and in-service training. In this paper, a Chief Education Officer comments on the implications of a changing society.

The form of the contribution which teacher education in any area should make to 'Teaching in a Multicultural Society' will reflect both the general responsibilities and duties of LEAs, and the particular characteristics of the community within the scope of an LEA. It is not possible, therefore, to reach a distinct LEA viewpoint which will be generally applicable. However, it is possible to suggest factors which Authorities may take into account in determining policies and in planning the allocation of resources to various activities.

There have been distinct trends in the pattern of educational programmes during recent years, affecting the ways in which educational provision is made for people of all ages: these changes have affected, and have been affected by the presence of, ethnic minority groups in the country. Where there has been some concentration of members of these groups in certain areas, attention has been focused on the need for special programmes to be provided by education and other services in those areas. During a similar period the multi-ethnic and multicultural nature of the UK population has been more clearly comprehended by policy makers and planners: in the education service, for example, it is more generally recognised that even where the proportion of ethnic minority pupils in a school is not statistically large, the curriculum should reflect the presence of minority groups in the community. If it is accepted that the curricular requirements of all pupils and students are affected to some extent by the change in the ethnic and cultural composition of the UK population, it would be helpful for all those concerned with the design of curricula to formulate and share their views.

Education services constitute one important part of

the contribution made by the community in meeting
needs of ethnic minority groups, but education and the
teaching process do not stand alone, unrelated to the
other aspects of social service which are made
available to individuals and groups. For teaching to
be effective, the total situation of the learner must
be understood, particularly by teachers, youth
workers, careers officers and others who give
professional services. LEAs are concerned with the
training, provision, re-training and support of
teachers and other professionals whom they employ in
implementing the services which are provided. LEAs are
responsible both for the quantity and the quality of
the service and for the staff who implement it.
Whatever demands local circumstances may make upon
their staff, LEAs are concerned that they are
adequately prepared for and supported in their work.
Solutions to problems frequently have resource
implications: there may be a need for more staff,
extended supporting facilities or other recurring
expenditure at an above-average level.

Through the curriculum a school or college sets out
its programme of learning, and indicates the standards
which it expects the learners to reach. The
curriculum indicates what is to be learnt and relates
this to the characteristics of the learners, which
includes their abilities, their attitudes and their
cultural backgrounds. For the curriculum of a school
to be regarded as satisfactory, it should be rewarding
and stimulating to the pupils and should provide them
with satisfactory opportunities for learning and
attaining objectives appropriate to their abilities.
The design of a satisfactory curriculum will avoid
obstacles to learning and enable most pupils to make
the progress of which they are capable.

In recent years, schools have become far more open to
the community at large and to parents in particular.
Teachers have welcomed the support and interest of
parents and many opportunities have occurred for home-
school links to be strengthened. The contribution
which parents, and the views of parents, make to the
running of schools and to the identification of the
objectives of schools can be considerable. However,
where cultural differences intervene, the
relationship between home and school may not be as
strong as would otherwise be the case. The pattern of
home-school activity can be affected greatly by the

various inherent attitudes of minority-group
families, and the views traditionally held in their
home countries of the place of education in society,
of the role of schools, and of the responsibilities to
be carried by teachers.

In considering the present position, it is important
to recognise the effects of two very significant
trends in recent years, namely (a), the limitations on
teacher training and teacher employment associated
with falling school rolls, and (b) the very
considerable restriction of expenditure within
education services. Both these factors will affect
increasingly the level of training possible for
teachers and other staff; the latter particularly
affects the level of resources which can be devoted,
especially in areas of concentration of ethnic
minority groups, to support additional measures to
overcome specific learning difficulties. With welcome
support from central Government funds for certain
programmes, LEAs have developed over recent years
substantial programmes to meet the needs of schools in
which pupils come from varying ethnic backgrounds. It
will not be easy for LEAs to expand these programmes
to any significant extent. Consequently, it is
essential to review priorities within existing
expenditure limits and to ensure the best use of
available resources. In developing the revised
arrangements for Local Authority finance which are
being introduced for the first time in the 1981/1982
financial year, account has been taken of the specific
needs of certain areas and the different levels of
service which they may be expected to provide; the
presence of minority groups and their needs for
education and other services have been recognised.

Multicultural Education For All Pupils

The last twenty years has seen a change in emphasis in
the area of multicultural education. We are now
concerned with teacher training for the whole
spectrum, ie for schools which are themselves
multicultural, and also for all schools in a
multicultural society. We have much to learn from the
example and experience of other countries. Sweden has
an action programme for multicultural education based
on the principles of equality of opportunity, freedom
of choice and partnership. Swedish schools have
already accepted the notion of multicultural education

for all pupils, and are now concentrating on the complexities of provision such as second and third stage language acquisition for minority group pupils. Many interesting developments in multicultural education may also be seen in Canada where, for example, the 'Heritage Language Programme' encourages a multilingual and multicultural approach, and essential support for class teachers is provided by official agencies through the production of curriculum papers and teaching material based on Canada's multicultural history.

In the UK many reports of value have been prepared, but frequently in fairly general terms. However, the 'Bullock Report' (1975) discussed the role of schools in a multicultural, multilingual society and offered many important guidelines. Indeed, it may be regretted that many of these recommendations have not been more actively pursued; if they had, the task now before us might be much smaller. Quite recently, the CRE/CNAA report on Race Relations and Equality of Opportunity has made recommendations on those aspects of some examinations which require attention if they are to be employed in a multicultural society. In 1977, the DES 'green paper' indicated the, then, Labour Government's positive support for the notion of education for a multicultural society; now, in the recent DES paper on The School Curriculum (1981), para 21 records the present Conservative Government's strong support for multicultural education in our schools. Some indication of the current need for progress to be made, in practice, is given by Little and Willey (1981) in their very recent report which concluded that few changes had occurred since the survey by Townsend and Brittan in 1972. Most of the recommendations by Little and Willey for action by LEAs will require for their implementation some form of teacher training. Needs have been documented, the policy statements have been made, now educationists must be engaged upon the issues with greater vigour than in the past.

To fulfil their role as the providers of suitable, efficient education, LEAs must continually review needs and provision. It is always necessary to establish priorities, and amongst these the education and training of the staff of the education service is essential: in-service training must be related to the teacher's task and rooted in the job teachers have to do. The role of the head of any school in this is crucial. It has been found that a realistic analysis of training needs emerges from a school-based, on-site approach to in-service training, and this may provide effective leads when conducted within multicultural schools and, also, in schools which see the need to develop multicultural approaches to the curriculum as a whole.

In the field of multicultural education, some immediate tasks which will involve teacher education and will concern LEAs as providers of the service, may be identified as follows:

(a) to assist awareness of pupils' cultural backgrounds as it affects learning and teaching

(b) to promote curriculum development for multicultural schools and for schools in a multi-ethnic society

(c) to provide information on teaching resources which reflect:

  - cultural backgrounds
  - multi-ethnic society
  - a multicultural heritage

(d) to develop programmes for mother tongue and culture maintenance

(e) to provide for training mother tongue teachers

(f) to devise plans for curriculum teaching in home languages and report on their implementation

(g) to provide guidance on the assessment of progress by ethnic minority pupils

(h) to prepare guidelines on multicultural perspectives across curriculum areas, leading to the drafting of schemes and pilot programmes

(i) to consider in all training programmes the multicultural aspects of education

(j) to evaluate learning materials for schools in a multicultural society

(k) to study schemes by which good home-school links have been established with ethnic minority parents, particularly in the case of younger pupils, and to develop guidelines

(l) to prepare programmes for teachers of English as a Second Language/Dialect, including factors such as aims, assessment, learning, teaching and resources

(m) to develop a broad approach to multiculturalism in education which teachers can develop, for seminar purposes, in their own sector or subject specialism

(n) to develop teaching support documents relating curricula to multicultural schools and to a multicultural society

(o) to explore, for all teachers, the relevance of the multi-ethnic society

(p) and to review examination syllabuses in all subjects and styles and modes, in relation both to a multi-ethnic society and to ethnic minority pupils.

Although not all these tasks can be accomplished within a short time, priorities may be identified and a phased programme devised. Many educationists in the UK have personal classroom experience of the important issues, and professional knowledge of curriculum design, linguistics, assessment etc. which would enable practical steps to be taken in several of the above areas within the foreseeable future.

REFERENCES

'Bullock Report' (1975), A Language for Life, HMSO

CRE/CNAA (1980), Race Relations & Equality of Opportunity, CNAA

DES (1977), Education in Schools: a Consultative Document, Cmnd.6869, HMSO

DES (1981), The School Curriculum, HMSO

Little, A. & Willey, R. (1981), <u>Multi-ethnic Education: the Way Forward</u>, The Schools Council

Townsend, H.E.R. & Brittan, E. (1972), <u>Organisation in Multiracial Schools</u> NFER

DISCUSSION

The paper on 'An LEA viewpoint' by Reg Hartles stimulated a good deal of discussion, both about existing provision and about possible strategies for further development and dissemination. Some of the main issues which were explored are summarised below.

1. ## Regional variations

   The widely varying patterns of ITT and INSET provision in multicultural education across the country was an issue which arose on a number of occasions during the seminar. During this discussion session the following suggestions were put forward:

   - a training the trainers programme for LEA advisers and staff in teacher education appears to be urgently needed, if there is to be more rapid progress in dissemination

   - while a number of LEAs have provided formal policy statements on multicultural education (for example, Bedford, Coventry, ILEA, Manchester), this has yet to be undertaken by the majority of Authorities

   - a centrally produced document for consideration by LEAs in areas with few ethnic minority pupils, outlining the issues and indicating strategies, would be helpful

   - there is as yet no national network of ITT and INSET teacher educators for whom multicultural education is a special interest, and whose purposes would be to exchange information, coordinate development, and disseminate ideas. On the other hand, an alternative might be to pursue 'permeation' through existing mechanisms.

2. ## Individual schools and LEAs

   Heads of individual schools who are sensitive to multicultural education can be a very positive factor in curriculum development; but in many cases, they require the support of the LEA. Elsewhere, the reverse situation may occur. How is this circle to be broken? the DES paper, *The School Curriculum* (1981), suggests that LEAs should frame policies for the school curriculum, and that "... every school should analyse its aims, set these out in writing, and regularly assess how far the curriculum within the school as a whole and for individual pupils measures up to these aims" (para.18). This would seem to present an appropriate opportunity for including multicultural education as part of the regular curriculum review.

3. <u>Existing curriculum development</u>

A number of participants called attention to the range and nature of LEA/nationally sponsored curriculum development work which relates both to special needs and also to multicultural education for all children, which is either already in use or in the process of preparation. The work of a number of individual LEAs was noted, as was the developing multicultural programme of the Schools Council, the Commission for Racial Equality, the Royal Society of Arts, and other bodies. However, there was felt to be a need for curriculum development in the different secondary school subjects, which would involve the subject advisers; and, again, the lack of a national focus of coordination and of dissemination of good practice was a point of discussion.

4. <u>The interprofessional aspect</u>

The identification of fellow professionals in the psychological, health, welfare, careers and probation services, who work closely with teachers and especially in inner urban areas was raised. To what extent does professional training for these supporting roles incorporate a multicultural perspective? How far are such colleagues included in INSET courses and school-based work for teachers, in this field?

5. <u>Equality of opportunity</u>

This underlying theme frequently found expression during the seminar. In this discussion session,

the point was made that the employment of ethnic
minority teachers by LEAs would be interpreted as
a clear indication of commitment to the principle,
quite apart from the obvious professional
advantages in schools.

Chapter Nine

AN HMI PERSPECTIVE

Ivor Ambrose

In this view from the Inspectorate, HMI Ambrose reports on a survey of multicultural provision in two-thirds of all initial training institutions in the public sector, in 1980.

Background

The task for teacher education, whether in respect of teaching in a multicultural society or any other aspect of teaching, is an ever-changing one, subject to changing national needs. Over the last fifteen years these have brought major transformations in teacher education.

In 1966, when initial training was expanding and there were nearly one hundred and seventy training establishments in the public sector of higher education in England, a survey by HMI investigated what colleges were doing about matters related to teaching in a multicultural society. At the time of the most recent survey on this subject, completed in 1980, there were only sixty-nine initial training institutions.

Much had happened in the intervening years besides the closures or amalgamations of about a hundred colleges. Reductions in student and staff numbers within institutions, a smaller range of main subjects and optional courses, new processes of validation, the growth of the BEd degree and the demise of the Teacher's Certificate, and the increase in the proportion of teachers entering service through the PGCE training route have all been major influences affecting teacher education. Diversified degree courses some involving joint teaching of BEd and other non-teaching degree students, modular structures, and consecutive patterns of training allowing for deferred commitment to teaching on the part of students, added further to the constraints of some institutions in the planning of their new BEd degrees.

Against this background of changes, provision for considering teaching in a multicultural society has had mixed fortunes. The 1966 survey referred to above showed that relatively few colleges of education had yet planned substantial courses concerning the education of children from minority ethnic groups or other aspects of the multicultural society. In the same year, a conference of HMI and representatives of interested bodies contributed to an increase in activity and provision. The National Council for Commonwealth Immigrants issued in thatyear a statement to the effect that (a) no college should contract out from the problems of immigration and the multicultural society, (b) all students should have the opportunity to study these problems during training, and (c) some students should be encouraged, through optional courses, to develop an advanced degree of knowledge and skill in this field.

By 1968/9 a further HMI enquiry showed that almost all colleges of education acknowledged their responsibility for matters concerning race relations, and that courses were being mounted dealing with the formation of attitudes or the acquisition of knowledge and skills. Thirty per cent of all colleges by this time were involved in both kinds of course, and a further sixty per cent were doing work on race relations or the education of immigrant children, or both, with at least some of their students.

In 1974 a Joint Working Party of the Association of Teachers in Colleges and Departments of Education (ATCDE) and the Community Relations Commission issued a report making a list of recommendations for teacher training. They dealt with the kinds of initial and in-service courses which ought to be offered, what their content might be, how institutions might provide tutorial and other resources for serving teachers, and how validating bodies might take into account multicultural society and ethnic minority considerations when judging the merits of syllabuses. With the demise of the ATCDE this useful dialogue closed, though the influence of the report lingered in colleges. More recently, however, the Commission for Racial Equality's paper, Schools and Ethnic Minorities issued in 1978, following a DES consultative document, stresses the importance of the part that should be played by initial training in relation to multicultural issues.

Other official reports (as indicated in Chapter One)
have added weight to these views, notably the
Parliamentary Select Committee on the West Indian
Community's report and the White Paper response to it
which not only drew particular attention to the need
for initial and in-service teacher education to take
account of ethnic minorities, but also led to the
establishment of the Rampton Committee of Inquiry into
the Education of Children from Ethnic Minority Groups.

The recent DES (1981) document, The School Curriculum,
and the HMI (1980) booklet, A View of the Curriculum,
both draw attention to the fact that our society has
become multicultural, and recent speeches by the
Secretary of State and Minister of State have
indicated the need for teachers to be better equipped
to respond to the problems and challenges raised by
education for life in a multicultural society. There
can be no doubt that a case has been made, which
demands a response both from initial and in-service
teacher education.

The Present Situation

During the course of 1979/80, an inspection exercise
was mounted which aimed at improving the
Inspectorate's knowledge of how institutions were
taking account, in initial training and in-service
courses for teachers, of matters relating to our
multicultural society. The exercise was in two parts.
The first was a largely factual inquiry in 46 of the
69 public sector institutions in England which offer
teacher education, i.e. a two-thirds sample. The
purpose of that inquiry was to bring up to date the
general picture of kinds of provision and approach
found in the Inspectorate's previous national
inquiries and in their more informal contacts. The 46
colleges were visited in HMI's normal course of work.
The second part of the exercise consisted of visits
lasting two or three days, by either two or three HMI,
to each of 12 of the 46 institutions, with the aim of
learning at first hand, and in some detail, about as
many aspects as possible of approaches to educational
issues concerning the multicultural nature of society.
In the selection of the 12 institutions, account was
taken of information from the first part of the
exercise which suggested where particular kinds of
provision might be found. Visits were also paid to
schools used by the 12 institutions to see students at

work either on teaching practice or in less formal contact with a school. The institutions consisted of four polytechnics, seven colleges of higher education, and one college concerned only with the initial preparation and in-service training of teachers. It is not possible in this chapter to comment in detail on the 12 institutions in the second part of the exercise. They did however shed useful qualitative light on the largely ·quantitative information gained in the first part.

It was quite clear from the sample of 46 that there is a very wide range of provision and practice within institutions of teacher training relating to education in a multicultural society. Recent changes associated with the reorganisation of teacher training have undoubtedly had adverse effects on this area of work in some instances, but have afforded new opportunities in others. The overall picture, however, is not a particularly bright one.

Without attempting to invest statistics with undue significance, the fact that in the view of staff concerned only 6 cases of improving provision were in prospect (and these were offset by 6 which had already reduced), 12 were uncertain and 22 probably unchanging, suggests a somewhat dormant state. Since some of the last group had little or no provision anyway, it is clear that the topic does not attract strong support in the planning of new courses within some institutions. Confirmation of this fact may be found in the opinion expressed in 21 cases that the issues of a multicultural society were not immediately relevant.

This widespread view of multicultural issues not being immediately relevant raises the conceptual question of what is commonly meant by 'education in a multicultural society'. Although some of the institutions expressed clear ideas, well related to the content of their courses, there was a very broad spectrum of views represented across the institutions, ranging from those case study examples to others which limited their consideration to the extent to which pupils from minority ethnic groups were to be found in teaching-practice schools, sometimes ignoring a substantial proportion within the locality. There is a clear need for teacher training institutions to reexamine both their concepts of education in a multicultural society and their courses, to see how they relate.

Staffing of this area of work reflected to some extent the conceptual problem. How should one staff such an ill-defined field which is neither a discipline nor a phase of education, and is multidisciplinary in nature though it is not self-evident which disciplines comprise it? Two attributes tended to identify staff, namely, expertise and commitment. The number of tutors with one of these, and the even smaller number with both, were not related to the size of the institution, the location of it or the work it was doing. Large polytechnics with only one lecturer in each engaged on this work, and much smaller colleges of higher education with three in each, illustrate the diversity. Further diversity in the form of subject expertise, brought to bear by tutors in such fields as English, sociology, religious studies, history, social anthropology, comparative education, curriculum theory, etc. served to indicate that the commitment of individual lecturers tended to determine the provision, rather than any overall view of what fields had a contribution to make.

Since most of the BEd degree courses in the 46 institutions were more or less concurrent, they offered a time span of three or four years in which education in a multicultural society could feature. This had enabled 30 of them to take some account of the topic at an appropriate point within the basic compulsory programme of professional training. Thus, some provision at least was made for all students in those contexts. The contrast with students training to teach by the PGCE route was striking, since only three such courses had an explicit compulsory element of education in a multicultural society, and only five others had incorporated reference to ethnic minority groups in school and society within basic educational or professional studies. The fact that a third of all the institutions train BEd students who, like the great majority of PGCE students, need take no account, during their preparation for teaching, of education in a multicultural society must be a matter for concern.

There is, however, in teacher training circles a widely held view that the student's course should not be overloaded, and some highly desirable elements, if they are to be given sufficient time and treatment to enable them to be done properly, can only be provided as options. Moreover, it may be argued that by choosing from a range of possible courses, a student comes more highly motivated to the one actually chosen. 'Better to do it well or not at all', is the essence of this approach.

Most institutions offered an optional course on education in a multicultural society within the BEd, thus enabling an interested student to pursue the topic in the absence of or in addition to any element in the basic education course. The fact that those aspects of this provision which concerned language acquisition, English as a second language, skills and understanding were in general more popular than cultural and social issues such as race relations which aimed at informing and shaping attitudes, is perhaps an indication of the utilitarian and pragmatic predilections of students in a situation of choice.

Options within the PGCE, though much less common, produced a similar pattern of choices on the part of students. Practical usefulness, especially for teaching practice purposes, again seemed to be a major determinant in a course being selected. And it is this very criterion which raises one of the main arguments against making provision for education in a multicultural society available solely through an option system, since so much depends on what other options are offered in competition with it. The usefulness of a course on slow learners, audio-visual aids or some such topic may well over-ride a student's interest in multicultural issues, as the anxieties of teaching practice draw near. Faced with some sets of options students may feel they have very little choice.

In five institutions, major study courses corresponding to a traditional main subject were offered which incorporated aspects of the multicultural society. Under titles such as world studies, community studies, urban studies etc., they provided scope for studying in depth a number of issues concerning ethnic minority groups (often groups with which links had been developed) inside a wider academic framework.

Questions as to what aspects of education in a multicultural society should be considered, avoided,

ignored or even sought after in a course, are worthy
of wide discussion. Whilst one would expect a
student's experience of multi-ethnic schools and
appropriate course preparation for this to be related
to the proximity of the training institutions to areas
of settlement by immigrant communities, this was by no
means universal. One-third of the institutions
offering courses on education in a multicultural
society did not bring students into sustained contact
with multi-ethnic schools or communities, even though
some were in areas of substantial ethnic minority
populations. Four others, however, situated far away
from any multi-ethnic schools, positively sought and
provided more distant fieldwork opportunities for
students in such schools and in ethnic minority
communities on a systematic basis.

In-Service Provision

In-Service training provision was to be found in fewer
than half of the institutions, and the fact that these
were located mostly in areas with multi-ethnic schools
indicates where teachers perceived their INSET needs
to be. The subject matter usually concerned education
in a school setting which is multicultural, rather
than the wider considerations of education in a
society which is multicultural.

There is clearly a relatively high demand for award-
bearing courses from those teachers in multi-ethnic
schools who are seeking to improve their knowledge and
professional skills to meet the particular demands of
their work. Questions of teachers' status, career
structure and the sheer worthwhileness of their
committing time to studying education in its
multicultural aspects, are closely related to
academically respectable qualifications being
available to them. But the predominance of award-
bearing courses does not stem solely from this source.
The institutions themselves often find them more
convenient to mount than shorter courses, which may be
regarded as the province of the LEA advisory services.
It would, however, be a pity if institutions
concentrated unduly on award-bearing courses to the
neglect of shorter ones which meet the needs of
teachers unable to commit themselves to long-term
advanced study. Indeed, the best examples of good
practice were to be found in cases where an
institution had developed a balanced programme of long
and short in-service course provision in close co-

operation with its Local Authority's advisory service in multicultural education.

Broad geographical areas remain where there is no provision within the notional two-ninths of resources available for in-service training, the majority of the institutions making no contribution, even where some aspects of education in a multicultural society feature in their initial training courses. This, together with relatively restricted coverage, noted above, arising from the narrow concentration by other institutions on factors relating to teaching in a multi-ethnic school, means that there is fairly scant treatment of social and cultural issues within in-service provision generally.

Evidence from the institutions showed that where good provision exists it has usually been achieved as a result of considerable effort. Institutional reorganisation and the validation of new courses have been the means of negotiating improvements in some courses. There has usually been apparent the strong influence of one or two key tutors with both personal commitment and the facility for involving others with different roles and expertise. Someone with a designated role such as 'co-ordinator of multicultural education' has often served a useful function, both as a source of knowledge and also in identifying and harnessing the collective and diverse strengths and resources of colleagues. At this time, when courses of teacher training are continuing to change with the progress of re-validation processes, it is worth remembering that the influence of one competent tutor with a specific responsibility in this area of work can be of exceptional significance.

Given a nuclear group of interested staff, provision certainly has benefited further by the setting up of organisational machinery for close co-operation, either formally or informally, through working groups and committees. The importance of such a structure could be detected in several institutions visited by the qualities of both academic content and practical work within the courses. Moreover some very significant staff development activity on education in a multicultural society was initiated by this means.

What of the Future?

Any consideration of the rationale and implementation
of multicultural education with reference to teacher
education needs to take account of the following
factors, among others:

1. The content of a course is the responsibility
    of the individual institution and its
    validating body.

2. The proportion of students qualifying for
    teaching through the PGCE route is growing,
    whilst the BEd proportion is reducing.
    Graduates in mathematics and science may teach
    without any initial training at all.

3. With a relatively static teaching force of
    over 400,000 and a need for little more than
    10,000 new entrants per year from training,
    initial courses, however good in quality, will
    not make a great impact on the total system
    quantitatively.

4. In-service provision must be the major area of
    concentration if practice within schools is to
    be significantly influenced.

5. Forms of in-service provision need to be
    explored which can be effective within the
    limits of continuing tight financial
    constraints.

6. There is evidence that the issues involved in
    teaching in a multicultural society are by no
    means clear either to teachers themselves or
    to teacher educators. There is at present
    insufficient dialogue.

REFERENCES

CRC/ATCDE (1974), Teacher Education in a Multicultural Society, CRE

CRE (1978), Schools & Ethnic Minorities, CRE

DES (1980), A View of the Curriculum, HMSO

DES (1981), The School Curriculum, HMSO

DISCUSSION

The final session which included a paper by HMI Ivor Ambrose and a brief commentary by HMI Eric Bolton, returned to the task for teacher education, considering in particular the problems of policymaking in a decentralised system. Main points as follows.

1. DES, LEAs and teacher education

    The point was made that central government has in recent years made a number of clear references to the educational needs of a multicultural society, and most recently in the DES paper, *The School Curriculum* (1981)*. In a decentralised system, it is now for LEAs, teacher educators and teachers to devise and implement appropriate professional responses.

    -   more LEAs might consider, for example, the drafting of a policy statement for their schools on the meaning of multicultural education, and on the kinds of curriculum development and staff development strategies which this implies. LEAs might similarly review their policies on appointments, including the staffing of advisory teams, and on secondment and release, as an indication of the importance placed upon multicultural education

    -   initial and in-service teacher educators need to define quite explicitly the essential professional characteristics required by those who teach, or wish to teach, in a multicultural society. They need to be adequately prepared, for example, for the diverse school populations they are likely to meet; they need to be led to a greater awareness of their own levels of intercultural prejudice; and they require techniques for taking account of a multicultural perspective in the teaching of their subject specialism.

---

* For example, in paras. 21, 27, 36, 49, 50.

2. Problems of initiation and coordination

Who takes a lead in a decentralised system? Who provides for an adequate flow of information? Who ensures a continuing dialogue among practitioners, trainers, employers and researchers respectively, and also a continuing dialogue between them? How is coordination achieved, so as to avoid too wide a variation in expertise among practitioners on the one hand, and too much duplication of effort among research and development agencies on the other? Seminar participants recognised the bureaucratic problems of a complex society and the ethical dilemmas of a social democracy, during this particular discussion. A number of specific suggestions were made:

- the need for 'training the trainers' courses for LEA advisers, and for lecturers in Colleges, Polytechnics and Universities involved in initial and in-service teacher education, was again raised

- the need for a centralised information agency was outlined. The DES was not thought appropriate; but in the absence of the former Centre for Advice and Information on Educational Disadvantage (- and the association with 'disadvantage' is arguable), a similar non-governmental body was needed to fill this role: the NFER? the Schools Council?

- it was generally felt that a new, specialised agency for initiating curriculum development and staff development in multicultural education was not desirable, and that permeation through existing agencies (teachers' unions and lecturers' associations, subject associations, validating bodies etc;), was a preferable strategy. Indeed, individuals through their membership of professional associations, school or college governing bodies, and validating committees could often exert a significant degree of influence

- a strategy which had proved effective in other areas of curriculum development had been to link innovative teachers with teacher educators. In this way, teacher educators may gain the immediacy of the classroom, and innovative practices can feed back into initial training; while teacher educators can contribute conceptual analysis and rationale, evaluation and dissemination to the process.

3. Change in initial and in-service teacher education

A number of issues on this theme were raised during the discussion, among them the following:

- teacher educators in ITT need to appraise their academic and professional courses, and to ensure that an informed sensitivity to cultural diversity is an integral part of their B.Ed./PGCE programmes for all students. It should not simply be offered through options; nor should it be left as a matter of conscience for individual students, but it should be regarded as a basic part of every young teacher's professional outlook and expertise

- just as the textbooks in use in schools are gradually coming under review, those used in teacher education also require re-appraisal. Few explicitly take note of the multicultural nature of British society, or make reference to the implications for teaching styles and curriculum content

- there is a need for a set of 'guidelines' on how initial and in-service teacher education should now proceed. What are the underlying principles, the aims and objectives which should inform our practice? What are the specifics relating to curriculum and organisation with which students should become acquainted? Which are the most relevant bibliographies, the most useful sources of teaching materials, and the most interesting examples of good practice?*

- it was noted that some past successful examples of curriculum development through INSET had occurred where in-service mechanisms had been linked with commercial publication (for example, in science, modern languages, mathematics and English). Health education had also successfully utilised an across-the-curriculum approach, and it may be that multicultural education might best proceed by becoming associated with the continuing debate on the curriculum.

---

* (Some work of this kind is currently being undertaken under the guidance of the CRE Advisory Group on Teacher Education. A range of relevant work is also being carried out by the Schools Council).

Chapter Ten

OVERVIEW

Maurice Craft

This concluding Chapter offers some personal reflections on the task for teacher education in the light of the seminar proceedings, touching on aspects of rationale, leadership, complexity, dialogue, expertise and structure.

The seminar was not concerned primarily with teaching in a multicultural society, but with the task for teacher education. So far, the introduction of multicultural perspectives into the initial and in-service training of teachers has been largely a matter of exhortation by those who have surveyed the front-line situation in the schools, and have reported that teachers need to be better prepared for work in multi-ethnic classrooms, and by educationists and others who perceive the contribution which might in this way be made to a harmonious and fulfilling social order. As yet there have been few systematic attempts in Britain to analyse the why, how and what, and to interpret this rationale in the light of the existing disposition of staff and other resources.

Rationale

The 'why' is the first and most fundamental question: on what basis, pragmatic or idealistic, is teacher education being asked to review its present provision? We have as yet no formulated analysis of the curriculum needs of a multicultural society and the implications for teacher education, although it is likely that several attempts will appear during the next year or two. This is plainly illustrated by the controversy over mother tongue teaching, and even more-so by any suggestion of bilingualism. As a society we are still unclear about our attitudes towards culture maintenance.

'How' in initial training for example, concerns the compulsory - core/option/permeation debate, and the detailed implementation of these strategies in a context of complex modular degrees and changing patterns of staffing and of student recruitment is also a large question. Perhaps a more determined attempt at tackling the question of staff expertise (a point returned to later) would ease a number of these 'logistical' problems by suggesting a variety of modes of permeation through what is taught at present.

'What' concerns the content of multicultural teacher education. Should this be mainly concerned with the acquisition of particular classroom skills for meeting special needs? Or more a matter of cultivating attitudes towards cultural diversity? Or should we make workshop introspection in the area of prejudice and discrimination the core of our work in teacher education? Another large question. Although little systematic work has yet been undertaken in any of these areas, these are the kinds of questions very familiar to teacher educators whose journals and conferences over the years have regularly agonised about means and ends, and about teacher effectiveness and its evaluation.

Leadership

The Nottingham seminar sought to make a small contribution to the exploration of these issues, and the papers and discussion seminars ranged widely across them. Given the limited time of a weekend event we were able to achieve no great depth, and inevitably suffered a certain amount of over-simplification of complex matters. On the other hand, it proved possible to avoid almost completely the polemics so often associated with work in this field, and also much of the cynicism. This was a gathering of experienced, knowledgeable and committed specialists, and while not without a lively scepticism, it generated much constructive discussion of the central policy issues involved. The question of national leadership, for example. It is a common experience for conference-goers to find that responsibility for the main problem under examination is quickly transferred to others outside the conference room, at an early stage in the proceedings. In educational gatherings it is usually the DES which is blamed for all failings, closely followed by 'ivory tower' academics, teacher trainers, and 'armchair critics' of all kinds.

What was apparent to many at this seminar, however, was the all round failure of the system in this case : central and local government, teacher educators and validators, schools and teachers. Individual examples of good practice were cited at each level; but clarity of purpose, rational planning, and imaginative implementation have been conspicuously absent. Much the same might be said of other educational developments, but the politically volatile nature of this field with its fearful potential for social conflict renders our failure the more alarming.

References to the need for a clearer lead from the DES about multicultural education in schools and in teacher education, have certainly been made down the years, and most recently by the Rampton Committee and by the House of Commons Home affairs Committee[1]. At the same time some very clear Government statements have now been made, including that by a DES Minister in April 1980[2], the Home Secretary in July 1980[3], and the DES curriculum paper in March 1981 (DES 1981a). If more LEAs were now to draw up policy statements on multicultural education, and if teacher trainers and validators were to apply a sharper eye to changing social needs we might begin to make up for lost time in those regions and institutions where little has happened. Initiatives in a field as diverse as this can arise anywhere in the system. Given the clear policy statements of the National Union of Teachers, for example, we may see more school-based experimentation, and particularly where staff development is concerned perhaps teachers will call upon the assistance of LEA advisory services and local teacher training institutions, without waiting for courses to be mounted.

---

[1] "We ... have the impression that the Department has in the past been more reticent in encouraging good practice in the field of ethnic minority education than in some other areas such as home-school liaison, curriculum reform or corporal punishment", (op.cit., para.132).

[2] Baroness Young, in an address to a CRE conference on education in a multicultural society, and quoted in a DES Press Notice on 19 April 1980.

[3] Mr. William Whitelaw, in an address to the Birmingham Community Relations Council.

Complexity

The complexity of the field is another aspect of the task for teacher education which concerned seminar participants. Organisationally, as I have suggested, responsibility for clarifying purposes and implementing policies is distributed throughout the system, and the political, diplomatic and resource implications are immense for those seeking change. But if we look again at the content of teacher education (the 'what' to which I referred earlier), this too can be a minefield. Take the 'special needs' approach, which is increasingly being thought of as rather limited: is this now completely dated? Are there no ethnic minority children experiencing continuing language problems, even in the second generation? Are the intergenerational problems of Asian adolescents in particular, or the alienation of minority teenagers in general, merely theoretical notions with no basis in reality? Are there not particular classroom skills, and strategies of home-school relationships, which could substantially influence the life-chances of individual minority pupils?

Currently more fashionable is an across-the-curriculum approach to sensitising initiates and serving teachers to cultural diversity, in whatever setting they will be working. Will this vitally important objective be achieved by modifications to existing syllabus content in all teacher education departments, without involving staff and students in an examination of their long-established assumptions; a matter of information input only? Even at that level, as Alan James has suggested in Chapter Six, there are no short-cuts to the elimination of defective teaching materials in a social democracy.

But if introspection is felt to go deeper and to be more effective, and the area of intercultural (not merely interracial) prejudice and discrimination is thought to be a third essential element in the modern curriculum for training teachers, what disciplines and techniques will we require in this? It is possible that the traditional professional and academic resources of educationists may not be sufficient. An interdisciplinary approach involving social psychologists and anthropologists may prove necessary, just as an interprofessional approach to in-service training in the area of home, school and community may need to be given more attention than it has attracted so far.

Dialogue

If a realistic sense of the multi-faceted nature of the problem was evident at the seminar, and a degree of scepticism about single-factor modes of analysis and simplistic 'solutions', the need for a fuller 'dialogue' was also apparent and was specifically highlighted by HMI Ivor Ambrose at the closing session. At every level, there needs to be a fuller exchange of views about the educational needs of a multicultural society. With the publication during 1981 of several major Reports[1], and a developing programme of work in multicultural education by the Schools Council, some active LEAs, and others, the dialogue may now be gathering pace. It is necessary in order to clarify definitions and assumptions, to refine ideas about implementation, to generate the necessary evaluation of what is done, and to help examples of good practice to become better known.

The information flow itself is an aspect of the dialogue which may also need attention. A new quarterly abstracting service is to appear in 1982[2] which will certainly be of help to trainers, but for news of developments on the ground there is as yet no successor to the nationally distributed newsletter on multi-ethnic education which was produced by the former Centre for Advice and Information on Educational Disadvantage. Any replacement would do well to sever the connection with disadvantage, for as suggested above, the implications of multicultural education are much broader.

---

[1] Schools Council (1981), DES (1981b) (the 'Rampton Report'), and House of Commons (1981a).

[2] *Multicultural Education Abstract*, published by Birmingham Polytechnic.

Expertise

Related to the need for dialogue is the available knowledge-base from which we must work in teacher education, and by this I mean the skills and awareness of lecturers, advisers and teachers' centre staff. Ideally, all teacher training institutions and every LEA should have someone on the staff who is au fait with current issues in multicultural education and who can mount courses or act as consultant. But in practice it might be the religious education adviser who is asked to look after this aspect in an LEA, or the sociology of education specialist in a College, Polytechnic or University department. It was therefore not surprising to find the need for training the trainers arising in many of the discussion sessions, and it is a primary recommendation of both the Rampton and House of Commons Reports (op.cit).

It is not uncommon nowadays, in my experience, to encounter goodwill and a willingness to respond in training institutions; but many institutions lack staff who are sufficiently knowledgeable or who possess relevant teaching experience, and who would be able to initiate courses or offer consultancy. In a contracting teacher education system such as we have at present, training the trainer is the only real alternative to the appointment of specialist staff.

Another aspect of the knowledge-base from which a multicultural perspective in teacher education may develop is the need for research and development work of a policy-oriented kind. Sample surveys of ITT lecturers and INSET advisers, for example, would give greater precision to a training-the-trainers initiative by pinpointing areas of need. Trialling and evaluating different modes of multicultural input would also be useful. Going further, it would be worth examining attitudes towards teaching as a career among ethnic minority sixth formers, for the intake is still quite limited.

Structure

The changed balance of teacher education must also now be a factor in any planning for a multicultural perspective at this level. Not only are far more student teachers taking the PGCE route compared with that of the B.Ed. degree, but there are far fewer young teachers entering the teaching force altogether.

The identified weakness in PGCE provision in respect of multicultural education must therefore command some importance in our planning; but overall, greater attention will now need to be given to in-service compared with initial training. The serious decline in resources allocated to INSET in the last few years - the closure of teachers' centres, the decline in full-time secondments and of supply staff to replace teachers on day-release courses, the reduction in course fees and travelling expenses - could hardly have come at a worse time from this point of view. But where schools, LEAs and training institutions work closely together progress should still be possible, and the fuller exploitation of school-based work will have advantages.

These are some personal reflections on the task for teacher education, in the light of the Nottingham seminar. It seemed a useful stocktaking, and it would be good to think that a similar gathering in three years' time would be likely to report a much improved picture with many varied examples of individual initiatives and developments. The rate of social, economic and political change in the world outside our classrooms and lecture rooms is such that we have little choice but to move with all possible speed.

APPENDIX A

The C.R.E. Advisory Group on Teacher Education

The Advisory Group was established to aid the
Commission in contributing to the development of a
greater sensitivity to the needs of a multicultural
society in both initial and in-service teacher
education. It has set up several Working Parties, each
with a particular area of concern, and has a
developing network of Regional Convenors whose role is
to facilitate relevant work in ITT and INSET. Its
current activities include the preparation of a policy
statement on teacher education in a multicultural
society, and it has a number of research and
development proposals in train.

The Advisory Group meets some six times a year under
the Chairmanship of Professor Maurice Craft of
Nottingham University. Its membership is as follows:

Mr B J Ashley
Director, School of Community Studies
Moray House College of Education

Ms J Barrow
Institute of Education
London University

Mr W Boaden
Formerly, Director
Centre for Educational Disadvantage

Professor L Cohen
Department of Education
Loughborough University

Professor M Craft
School of Education
Nottingham University

Mr C T Crellin
School of Education
Middlesex Polytechnic

Mr F Cummins
Headmaster
Thomas Telford High School
West Bromwich

Professor S J Eggleston
Department of Education
Keele University

Mr M Feeley
Adviser for Multicultural Education
Coventry LEA

Dr P Figueroa
Department of Education
Southampton University

Professor R Giles
Department of Educational Studies
Birmingham Polytechnic

Dr J Gundara
Coordinator, Multicultural Centre
Institute of Education
London University

Mr R J Hartles
Chief Education Officer
London Borough of Ealing

Mr H L Hough
Headmaster
Hilton Lane Primary School
Manchester

Ms I Morrison
Warden, Lewisham Teachers' Centre
ILEA

Mr T Mukherjee
Senior Lecturer in Education
Southlands College

Mr J Parr
Head, Community and Youth Studies
Westhill College

Mr E Robinson
Principal
Bradford College

Mr J Singh HMI
Department of Education and Science

Professor M Skilbeck
Director of Studies
The Schools Council

Ms N Whitbread
School of Education
Leicester Polytechnic

APPENDIX B

Seminar Participants

Members of this invited seminar included teachers from primary, secondary and further education; LEA advisers and Teachers' Centre wardens, and members of H.M. Inspectorate; teacher trainers, and academic and other specialists in the field of multicultural education; and staff of the Commission for Racial Equality.

Mr I Ambrose, HMI, Department of Education and Science

Mr B J Ashley, Director, School of Community Studies, Moray House College of Education (Commissioner CRE)*

Mr A Awan, Schools Inspector, City of Birmingham LEA

Ms J Barrow, Research Fellow, Department of Comparative Education, London University Institute of Education*

Mr E J Bolton HMI, Educational Disadvantage Unit, Department of Education & Science

Mr W Boaden, formerly Director, Centre for Advice & Information on Educational Disadvantage, Manchester*

Mr T Burgess, Lecturer in Education, Department of English, London University Institute of Education

Mr G Burrows, Adviser, Bedfordshire LEA, Chairman, National Association for Multiracial Education

Mr T Carter, Teacher, Brooke House School, Hackney, London

Rabbi D S Charing, Director, Jewish Education Bureau, Leeds

Mr J Chandley, Inspector of Schools, Nottinghamshire LEA

Mr D Cherrington, Reader in Education, Centre for Advanced Studies in Education, Birmingham Polytechnic

---

* Member of CRE Advisory Group on Teacher Education

Dr J Cheshire, Lecturer in Linguistics, Department
of Linguistics, Bath University

Mr R Clamp, Senior Lecturer, Airedale & Wharfedale
College of F.E., Leeds

Mrs A Z Craft, Senior Research Officer, Research
Team, The Schools Council

Professor M Craft, Head, Colleges Division, School
of Education, Nottingham University*

Mr C T Crellin, Principal Lecturer in Education,
B.Ed. Course Coordinator, Faculty of Education,
Middlesex Polytechnic*

Mr F Cummins, Headteacher, Thomas Telford High
School, W. Bromwich (Commissioner CRE)*

Mr G S Dhaliwal, Immigrant Liaison Officer, Bradford
LEA

Mr W O B Doherty, Headteacher, Linden Secondary
School, Gloucester

Mr L Duncan, Deputy Headteacher, Sidney Stringer
Secondary School, Coventry

Professor S J Eggleston, Head, Department of Education,
Keele University*

Mr M R Feeley, Adviser for Multicultural Education,
Coventry LEA*

Dr P Figueroa, Lecturer in Education, School of
Education, Southampton University*

Mr E Gaffikin, Vice-Principal, Brixton College
of F.E.

Dr P Ghuman, Lecturer in Education, Department
of Education, University of Wales (Aberystwyth)

Professor R Giles, Centre for Advanced Studies
in Education, Birmingham Polytechnic*

Mr D Goddard, Warden, Enfield Teachers' Centre,
Middlesex LEA

---

* Member of CRE Advisory Group on Teacher Education

Mr J D Green, Senior Lecturer in Education, Urban
    Studies Centre, College of St Mark and St
    John, London E2

Mr R E Grinter, Senior Lecturer in Education,
    School of Education, Manchester Polytechnic

Ms A Hayler, Assistant Teacher, Lucas Vale Infants
    School, London SE8

Mr R J Hartles, Chief Education Officer, Ealing LEA*

Mr M Hobbs, Director, B.Ed. (Multicultural Studies),
    Birmingham Polytechnic

Ms D V Hoffman, ESL Organiser & Tutor, Charles
    Keene College of F.E., Leicester

Mr H Hough, Headteacher, Hilton Lane Primary School,
    Manchester*

Mr A James, Principal Lecturer in Education, Derby
    Lonsdale College of Higher Education

Ms D Joslin, Warden, English Language Resources
    Centre, Southampton

Mr S Kalsi, Lecturer in Education, Faculty of
    Contemporary Studies, Bradford College

Mr A R Kaushal, Senior Lecturer in Education,
    Department of Community Relations, Edge Hill
    College of Higher Education, Ormskirk, Lancs

Ms G Klein, Librarian & Resources Adviser, Centre
    for Urban Educational Studies, ILEA

Ms C S Lerch, Intercultural Education Coordinator,
    U.S.A.

Dr J Lynch, Head of Teaching Studies, Faculty
    of Education, Sunderland Polytechnic

Mr P J Matthews, Headteacher, St Chrysostoms C of E
    Primary School, Charlton-on-Medlock, Manchester

Dr D Milner, Senior Lecturer in Social Psychology,
    Polytechnic of Central London

---

*   Member of CRE Advisory Group on Teacher Education

Mr T Mukherjee, Senior Lecturer in Education,
Southlands College, Roehampton Institute
of Higher Education*

Ms L O'Dwyer, Assistant Secretary, Royal Society
of Arts, London

Mr T M Ottevanger, Assistant Education Officer
(Multiracial education), Ealing LEA

Mr W Prescott, Senior Lecturer in Education, Faculty
of Educational Studies, The Open University

Professor J Rex, Director, SSRC Research Unit
in Ethnic Relations, Aston University

Mr K Richards, Senior Lecturer in Education, Department
of Education, Trent Polytechnic

Mr J C Robottom, Education Officer, Midland Division,
B.B.C.

Dr S Singh, Inspector of Schools, ILEA

Mr A Stibbs, Lecturer in Education, School of
Education, Leeds University

Miss L Thomas, Headteacher, Wilberforce Junior
School, Kilburn, London W10

Mr H Tomlinson, Headteacher, Birley High School,
Manchester

Dr S Tomlinson, Lecturer in Education, School
of Education, Lancaster University

Mr A Tosi, Lecturer in Department of Modern Languages,
Oxford Polytechnic

Mr H E R Townsend, formerly Senior Research Officer,
NFER, and Head of Education, Adelaide College
of Advanced Education, S.Australia

Mr B O Turner, County Adviser, Lancashire LEA

Dr G Verma, Senior Lecturer in Education, Postgraduate
School of Studies in Research in Education,
Bradford University

---

*   Member of CRE Advisory Group on Teacher Education

Mr C Vaughan, Warden, Gravesend Teachers' Centre, Kent

Mr J White, Headteacher, Uplands Junior School,
    Leicester

Dr R Willey, formerly Senior Research Officer,
    Goldsmiths' College, London University

Ms Yap Hi Chu, Lecturer in Social Studies, North
    London College of F.E.

Commission for Racial Equality

Mr C Robinson, Deputy Chairman

Mr H Lashley, Senior Education Officer, Public
    & Community Services Section

Ms L McWatt, Higher Executive Officer, Equal
    Opportunities Division

Ms Ming Tsow, Higher Executive Officer, Public
    & Community Services Section

Mr S Williams, Senior Research Officer,
    Research Section

---

*   Member of CRE Advisory Group on Teacher Education

INDEX